RIDING A STRAIGHT AND TWISTY ROAD

RIDING A STRAIGHT
AND
TWISTY ROAD

Motorcycles, Fellowship, and Personal Journeys

James Hesketh

CENTRAL RECOVERY PRESS

CENTRAL RECOVERY PRESS

Central Recovery Press (CRP) is committed to publishing exceptional materials addressing addiction treatment, recovery, and behavioral health care, including original and quality books, audio/visual communications, and web-based new media. Through a diverse selection of titles, we seek to contribute a broad range of unique resources for professionals, recovering individuals and their families, and the general public.

For more information, visit www.centralrecoverypress.com.

Central Recovery Press, Las Vegas, NV
© 2011 by Central Recovery Press

ISBN-13: 978-1-936290-05-5 (paper)
ISBN-10: 1-936290-05-7

17 16 15 14 13 12 11   1 2 3 4 5

Publisher: Central Recovery Press
             3371 N. Buffalo Drive
             Las Vegas, NV 89129

Images on pages 28, 40, 118, 126, 138, 162, 172, 182, 190, and 212 ©iStockphoto.com/pubily, used by permission.

Editor's Note: CRP offers a diverse selection of titles focused on recovery, addiction treatment, and behavioral health care/relationship topics. The experiences and opinions expressed in this book are those of the author only. To protect their anonymity, some of the names of people and institutions have been changed.

Cover design and interior by Sara Streifel, Think Creative Design

Dedicated to every rider
who has stopped to help someone
broken down on the side of the road.

CONTENTS

THE TIMES

IN THE 1969 FILM *Easy Rider,* Peter Fonda and Dennis Hopper ride motorcycles across America then blast off the silver screen to forever live in our collective consciousness as Captain America and sidekick Billy. Some called them bikers; others called them hippies. They didn't fit neatly into either stereotype, but whatever they were, they presented a new face of America's vision of freedom—a freedom fueled by drugs, narrated by rock and roll, and lived from the saddle of customized, chrome-laden Harley-Davidsons.

In its day, *Easy Rider* was a powerful and enigmatic film for a restless generation. Today, viewed through eyes four decades older, it's a cultural demarcation point between the hectic culture of the sixties and the hedonistic seventies. *Easy Rider* is a motorcycle movie and it's a drug movie, and in both those areas there is a story of before *Easy Rider* and after *Easy Rider.*

THE STAGED PHOTO THAT STARTED IT ALL—HOLLISTER 1947

Prior to *Easy Rider,* motorcycle movies were sensationalized tales of wild, senseless mayhem. Motorcycle riders were depicted as hoodlums and bikes were their vehicles of destruction. Portrayed as outlaw motorcycle gangs in popular media, bikers would ride into a small, innocent, peace-loving town and in a drunken frenzy destroy the idealized "life behind the white picket fence" dream that America was so desperate to believe in. Young girls felt threatened. Old men got killed. Churches were burned and businesses destroyed.

That wasn't the reality of motorcycling, but it was a general public perception. Marlon Brando starred in the first "biker" movie, *The Wild One.* Released in 1953 it was based on a sensationalized motorcycle rally in Hollister, California over Fourth of July weekend in 1947. A reporter staged outlandish photographs, one of which appeared in *Life Magazine*, that depicted the weekend gathering as a full-fledged riot. This gave birth to the iconic stereotype of the outlaw American Biker. The two other most notable pre-*Easy Rider* biker movies were *The Wild Angels* with Peter Fonda and *Hells Angels on Wheels* with Jack Nicholson, both representative of dozens of movies of that genre, which have more in common with modern horror movies than the reality of motorcycling. The opening credits of *The Wild One* even carry a public warning.

Of course there were members of motorcycle clubs who did their best to live that image. But the majority of riders were only interested in getting out and experiencing the freedom of the open road. The one-percenter label—according to popular lore but never confirmed by the American Motorcyclist Association (AMA)—was adopted from a statement by an AMA spokesman who said, "Ninety-nine percent of all motorcyclists are law-abiding citizens, and the last one percent are outlaws."

In its original context, the term "outlaw motorcyclist" did not mean they were criminals. The AMA was the official sanctioning body for all motorcycle races and rallies. Any club that was not a member of the AMA, or held an event that wasn't sanctioned by the AMA was labeled outlaw. Many riders took pride in being outsiders and embraced the outlaw biker image but didn't engage in illegal activity (other than maybe drinking a few too many beers or riding a bit too fast).

Alongside *Easy Rider*, two shows featuring motorcycles were broadcast on television during that closing year of the freewheeling sixties. In *Then Came Bronson,* a brooding, burned out reporter from San Francisco hit the road on his Harley-Davidson Sportster as a modern-day television cowboy improving the lives of troubled folks each week. And on the wholesome front, *Marcus Welby, MD* had a young assistant who rode a Triumph motorcycle on his rounds, back when TV doctors still made house calls. Through the taming of the biker image in popular media and the proliferation of modern dependable bikes from Japan in the early seventies, motorcycling started to become socially acceptable.

Motorcycling changed forever in 1969 with the introduction of Honda's CB750. In one way or another, almost every rider on the street today owes something to that bike. Unlike the big, heavy Harleys the bikers rode; the faster, high-performance, more nimble but finicky British motorcycles; or the small Japanese bikes available till then, the Honda 750 was clean, quiet, fast, easy to ride, and most importantly, dependable. At last the average person who was not interested in "image" could buy a respectable motorcycle to ride as a workday commuter, a weekend escape vehicle, or a cross-country touring machine. The public perception of motorcycling slowly began to change. Soon the Japanese big four—Honda, Kawasaki,

Suzuki, and Yamaha—were supplying bikes for riders who didn't fit the biker image.

The attitude toward drugs was changing then also. In the sixties drug use had a social purpose. On a cultural level, for a rebellious generation drugs became the equivalent of the secret handshake its parents used at lodge meetings—a form of identity. Drug use, as reflected in *Easy Rider*, was just a part of life, like food for the body or gas for the motorcycles. It was a tool of personal freedom for the "do your own thing" generation. As a closing chapter of the sixties, it was becoming a part of popular culture and gaining mainstream social acceptability. But as an opening chapter for the decade that followed, it foreshadowed a failed experiment in individual freedom.

In 1970 the Grateful Dead sang

What in the world ever became of sweet Jane?

She lost her sparkle, you know she isn't the same

Livin' on reds, vitamin C, and cocaine,

*All a friend can say is "Ain't it a shame?"**

By the beginning of the eighties, we knew we couldn't continue to just say "Ain't it a shame?" The drug use tolerated under the banner of "do your own thing" was destroying too many people and taking too many lives. We had to tell sweet Jane, "You need help." The Age of Aquarius morphed into the Age of Recovery. That's where the true idealism of the sixties lives—people taking care of each other, loving each other, and helping each other only because they need help and love and to be taken care of. Our survival depends on that.

*Reprinted by permission of Ice Nine Publishing

As Bill W discovered back in 1935 with the founding of Alcoholics Anonymous, recovery works because we are brought together through our shared vulnerability. The group's strength becomes the individual's strength. It's the shared experience and fellowship of twelve-step programs that gives many addicts a chance to change their lives.

Motorcyclists also have a shared experience and vulnerability that makes every rider a member of a special fellowship.

This is a fellowship, a brotherhood, a sisterhood of riders who are bound together by a desire to get out on a motorcycle—to be alone with their thoughts, to make friends with the road, the wind, the weather, the countryside, and each other.

Motorcycle riders are motion addicts. And only other riders truly understand the affliction. There is a common thread that binds all riders together: a desire to hear the music of the road. The motorcycle is the instrument that allows the tune to play inside of the rider's helmet. Members of the fellowship understand this. But not everyone wants to hear the same tune. Some riders don't hear the music unless they are on a long, straight, empty back road on a crotch rocket with the speedometer hitting the triple digits. For others it means finding the sound of solitude that comes from being out on the road for weeks at a time on a touring bike, exploring new country and discovering a perfect, isolated camping spot a half-tank away from the nearest sign of civilization. Still others prefer the sound of rock-and-roll thundering out of exhaust pipes on a warm evening while cruising on a shiny, chrome-laden, custom-painted Harley. And others join motorcycle clubs for the safety and camaraderie that only a symphony played by a well-tuned group of like-minded friends can provide.

But no matter which song a rider prefers, he understands the music. He understands what it means to be a motorcyclist and lives for the fellowship of the road.

For a rider, motorcycling is a celebration of life—and for those who have lived through the desperation of addiction every ride is an affirmation, a commitment, and an enhancement of a regained life.

THE RIDER

IT GETS REAL BUSY learning a new turn at a new racetrack. It can be terrifying if you get it wrong, and painful and expensive if you get it real wrong. But when you get it right for the first time it's an indescribable high. One that would be worth savoring, but at one hundred miles per hour you don't have any time for reflecting and savoring—you're too busy setting up for the next corner.

During the last practice session of my first race weekend I finally got one turn right. Turns six and seven at Homestead-Miami Speedway are taken as a single sweeping right-hander. A short straight connects two tight curves about a hundred yards apart, which makes it a big, fast, wide U-turn.

I'm in fifth gear coming into the turn. Downshifting to third while hard on the brakes, I spot my entry point, lean the bike over, and begin smoothly accelerating into the turn. Strafing the apex of turn six, the hard plastic protector on my knee scraping the track's surface, I twist the throttle, speed up, and swing wide to the outside edge of the track before continuing the arc back to the inside of turn seven. Shifting up to fourth while exiting the turn, I speed down the straight heading to turn eight. It was smooth, fast, comfortable, and good.

Then I had one of those magic moments when my body and mind come into sync, and that one nanosecond of sensation imprints itself forever in my memory.

I can conjure up that moment whenever I think of that turn on that December afternoon. In my memory is forever stored the roar of the exhaust and the power of the motorcycle's engine beneath me. I can picture the yellowish-orange tinge in the color of the late afternoon light and feel the coolness of the wind as it found every gap in my leathers. I still smell the sweet scent of the burnt race fuel from the little two-stroke bike that came through the turn ahead of me. I remember feeling absolutely perfect.

I imagine others have similar memories of extraordinary experiences: Mountain climbers may be able to recall conquering a difficult peak in the same way. A poet might be able to place himself in the exact state of mind he was in when he got a line right after struggling with it for weeks or months, and his soul let him know it was happy with the result. An athlete probably relives breaking a long-standing record with as much intensity.

For a motorcyclist those moments only come through a mating of rider, machine, and motion. I've got a few others; they are rare and precious and only happen by chance under special circumstances. One came to me while watching a sunset in West Texas after a thirty-six-hour marathon ride from Miami on my way out to California for a motorcycle rally. Another happened the day I rode my first motorcycle back in 1975, a Honda 360 I bought new before moving on to a chopped Triumph a couple years later.

Why do motorcycles do it for me—for us? I don't know and probably never will fully understand. I never had a chance to ride a bike until I had my first job out of high school and was ready to move out of my parents' house. Motorcycles were not allowed under their roof. I only know that from my earliest memories I was obsessed. As a kid I had pictures of motorcycles and posters from motorcycle movies tacked up on every inch of wall space in my room. I read every magazine and book I could find about bikes.

LATE SEVENTIES—MY CHOPPED TRIUMPH BONNEVILLE
LOOKED GOOD BUT WAS HELL TO RIDE

One of the first books I read as a preteen was Hunter Thompson's *Hell's Angels*. The story about the bikers was fascinating, but what really grabbed my interest were the final few pages of the book where he describes a high-speed midnight run down the Pacific Coast Highway south of San Francisco on a British BSA motorcycle.

Thompson concludes this passage with a few brief sentences about "The Edge." As he puts it, The Edge is that place just beyond that frantic all-consuming rush where a rider pushes his and his bike's ability to the limit. Some riders push over The Edge and travel off to eternity, whatever that may be. Others pull back at the last minute, just before the tires lose grip, just before they can't lean into the curve that essential additional degree to make it through, just before entering eternity. And they live to test themselves another day.

Those feelings of perfection I achieved in turns six and seven while practicing for my first motorcycle race, on the road riding cross country, and on my first ride are all on the road to The Edge. But I've never felt the need to push myself physically all the way; I've always pulled back.

That feeling of perfection is so seductive that I found cheats in my pursuit of it. Sometimes when perfection was just out of reach, a toke, a drink, a hit, a shot, or a line could get me there. And in moderation there probably wouldn't have been anything wrong with that. But somewhere along the way the cheats became more important than the pursuit, and I got lost in all those tokes, drinks, and hits. Even though my body didn't go over The Edge, the important parts of me—my self-esteem, my spirit, my ability to live without the shortcuts did. I couldn't pull back. I eventually came to depend on the shortcuts as a substitute for life's real victories. I even quit riding motorcycles for a number of years.

COMING INTO TURN ONE WHILE PRACTICING
FOR MY FIRST RACE AT DAYTONA

I reached bottom in 1983 and found recovery through a twelve-step program. It took a few years before I started riding again, and when I did it was more than a means of transportation and a hobby—it became an essential element of my life. Since then I've put a couple hundred thousand miles behind my taillight and have ridden through all the forty-eight contiguous states, Eastern Canada, Northern Mexico, and made a trip to ride in Italy. I began racing a few years ago at the age of fifty. That's one way of celebrating my life and my recovery.

I've found a huge community of clean and sober riders. Many belong to clubs, some are racers, and others just ride independently. We all share a need to get out and explore the open road (or racetrack) on two wheels. And we find a common interest in sharing our recovery and passion for riding with like-minded souls.

This book is a celebration of those lives, written for and by riders who have known desperation and now share the fellowship of the road and of recovery.

NOTE: In the summer of 2010 I needed time to work on some personal issues and headed out on the road in search of whatever it was that was missing in my life. Motorcycles are good for that. There is a popular T-shirt that reads, "You never see a motorcycle parked outside of a psychiatrist's office." This ride was a long, rolling personal therapy session that brought insights I never would have realized at home (or in a shrink's office). My journey brought me close to many of my brothers and sisters in recovery all across the country who, whether they know it or not, helped me on my journey. Many of those people I met and write about in this book have contributed their own stories of motorcycling and recovery. Those personal stories are interwoven into my narrative.

THE RIDE

1

"WELCOME HOME."

The greeting was symbolic, but it drove straight into me. Those words and the firm handshake coming from a man I'd never seen before, in a house I'd never visited before, put a huge lump in my throat and brought tears to my eyes.

It's the fourth morning of an open-ended motorcycle trip, and I'm at Dr. Bob's house on a hot Sunday morning in an old neighborhood in Akron, Ohio. This is where Bill W and Dr. Bob founded Alcoholics Anonymous, the fountainhead of all twelve-step programs, where alcoholics, drug addicts, gamblers, overeaters, and millions of others have found freedom and recovery from old, painful, destructive, and desperate attempts at life.

I'm on a ride that will eventually take me from my home in Miami out to the Black Hills Motorcycle Rally in Sturgis, South Dakota, on

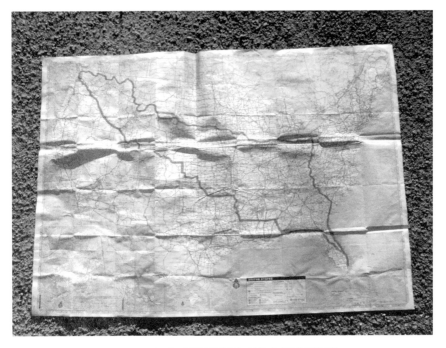

MY ROUTE—THREE WEEKS AND 9,500 MILES

to Seattle, and back home through Colorado. I've already put fifteen-hundred miles on my bike, and the number on the odometer will increase by another eight thousand before I roll into my driveway again three weeks from now.

This is a trip of rediscovery, a recommitment to my recovery, and a chance to head out onto the open road. It's a change of inertia. You know Newton's First Law of Motion—an object at rest tends to remain at rest and an object in motion tends to remain in motion.... Well, I've been at rest for too long now. I've been sitting still, or maybe even going backward, emotionally, mentally, physically, and spiritually for a number of years now, and I can't think of a better way to get all those areas of my life into motion than to climb on a motorcycle and get some wind up my nose.

I call the first leg of any worthwhile motorcycle trip from South Florida the penalty phase. Maybe I've ridden up and down the full length of Florida too many times on various trips and become jaded, but to me it's just a lot of long, hot, straight, flat, miles on a crowded road full of impatient drivers. There are three main highways that run up through Florida: Interstate 95, the Florida Turnpike, and Interstate 75. These three mostly indistinguishable highways are the most boring roads I've had the pleasure of enduring—just monotonous hours of sitting in the saddle, twisting the throttle to put miles behind the taillight and cross into Georgia where the promise of curves and hills lies ahead. Riding the interstates in Florida is like sitting down alone to drink a case of non-alcoholic beer. The bottle feels familiar in your hand and the taste is similar to the real thing, but you're going to get bloated and sick before you get a buzz.

I'd rolled out of my driveway early on the Thursday afternoon before my visit to Dr. Bob's house, after packing my bike while waiting for the morning thunderstorms and rush hour traffic to dissipate. Although the Weather Channel predicted I'd be riding in rain in most of the day, I chose to wear my ventilated riding suit without the waterproof liner because of the heat and humidity. The roads were wet, but I didn't hit any rain until just south of Daytona. By that time, the cooling effect of the rain felt good, and the reduced visibility and added attention that riding in rain requires was actually a welcome diversion from the droning pace of the interstate. I snapped out of my highway hypnosis and rode through heavy rain into Jacksonville. Luckily, my late start kept me out of the evening rush hour traffic through the city; I passed through Jacksonville and out of Florida into Georgia as the sun came out again, and I watched my shadow grow long and dance on the cars in the slow lane and the tall weeds of the shoulder on my right. Even though I-95 is still mostly flat and straight in South Georgia, riding north of the state line is as different from riding in Florida as peaches are from oranges. The land opens up and the highway passes through grassy marshland and crosses over tidal rivers on tall bridges before trading the faint scent of coastal waters for the distinctive smell of pine forests as the highway took me inland and away from the coast.

A lot gets said and written about the difference between riding a motorcycle and driving a car. Drivers usually defend their vehicle of choice by stating how dangerous motorcycles are and how exposed riders are. Ironically, the greatest danger to motorcyclists usually comes from inattentive drivers, whom we often call "cagers," because they're stuck in a cage while we're out in the open, fully experiencing the environment we ride through. Drivers are observers; riders are participants.

Riders usually cite the "feeling of freedom" as their best reason to ride. Although he wasn't talking about motorcycles, Thomas Jefferson said, "The price of freedom is eternal vigilance...." Riders understand Jefferson's words—not in the political context he was speaking of, but for our very survival in a hostile environment full of obstacles and hazards that could turn a pleasant ride into a nightmarish tumble across the pavement in the blink of an eye.

As I was looking forward to some of the day's oppressive heat dissipating along with the fading sunlight, I suddenly caught a whiff of hot rubber. Instantly alert, I scanned the road ahead of me and noticed a puff of smoke coming from the rear tire of a tractor-trailer rig immediately in front of my bike. Swerving into the lane to my right while accelerating, I managed to get even with him before his tire blew, throwing large chunks of heavy rubber and shards of steel into the space where I had just been riding. At best I would have ridden through a shower of hot rubber and steel; at worst my bike's wheel could have caught the road gator (as the sections of thrown-off tire treads are called), and I could have gone down. Constant vigilance—it's a good thing. I survived that moment of danger and got to ride on and enjoy more miles of freedom.

Crossing into South Carolina well after dark I began looking for a place to pitch my tent. I'd already ridden close to six hundred miles and was getting tired. My hope had been to make it to Asheville, North Carolina, where I was to meet some friends for lunch the next day, but I didn't feel like pushing another couple hundred miles on my first day out. Having no luck finding a campground near the interstate, I settled for a cheap motel near the town of St. George, hit McDonald's for a quick burger, tended to the bike, called my wife, checked the next day's weather on the local news, crawled into bed, and slept like a baby.

Morning found me loading the bike before the sun rose above the treetops on the far side of the motel's parking lot. I checked the free continental breakfast in the lobby and decided to hold out for an Egg McMuffin somewhere down the road. Pulling onto the interstate, my left turn signal wasn't working; I began looking for an auto parts store where I could get a replacement bulb. After trading northbound I-95 for northwest-bound Interstate 26, I spotted a "travel plaza" with a McDonald's restaurant. Perfect, I could fix the bike, fill the tank, and eat in one fell swoop.

Before my trip ended, I learned to both loathe and love these ubiquitous travel plazas that have sprouted up alongside interstate highways in the way that the greenest grass always grows over the septic tank. It would be possible to drive across the entire US of A without ever getting further away from the highway than a truck stop. Many of them have motels on-site. All have—besides the obvious fuel pumps—restaurants and stores with everything a traveler needs for a fast, sterile trip from one coast or border to another. Most have mechanics on duty, showers, entertainment centers and lounges, and, out west where gambling is legal, casinos. They are clean, safe, and predictable.

That's the last thing I'm looking for when on a motorcycle trip.

I prefer to stay on two-lane back roads where I may have a chance to catch a glimpse of "the real America," find cozy campgrounds near quiet rivers or forests, and stay at the occasional ma and pa motel. But the interstates and travel plazas are a necessary compromise in any adventure, especially when it's important to cover a lot of miles in a short time.

After filling my gut at McDonald's—where I discovered some locations now charge a quarter for a glass of tap water—filling my tank with premium, and replacing the burnt-out signal bulb, I was back on the road heading for Asheville. Gradually, the highway began to follow the contour of the land, and I had to lean into some gentle curves and modulate the throttle when climbing up grades and coasting down small hills. Once I got into North Carolina and reached the Blue Ridge Mountains and crossed over the 2,100-foot Eastern Continental Divide, I felt like I had finally escaped the flatland and my ride had really begun.

I only had three planned stops on this trip; lunch with a couple old friends from my early days of recovery who now live in Asheville was the first. Pulling in to the historic downtown area just before noon, I immediately understood why Asheville constantly gets top ratings in various national polls: *Rolling Stone* calls it the "New Freak Capital of the US," and *Modern Maturity* lists it as one of "The 50 Most Alive Places to Be." Any city that's touted by both *Rolling Stone* and *Modern Maturity* as a top place to live has something special going for it. A huge arts and vibrant music scene and access to the wilderness of the Blue Ridge Mountains brings free spirits, former hippies, nature freaks, and young kids seeking a taste of sixties idealism flocking to this bastion of open-mindedness nestled in the middle of southern Bible Belt conservatism.

My friend and former riding buddy Jack escaped the craziness of Miami for the serenity of life in the mountains about ten years ago. Jack doesn't ride anymore; he traded the open road for family life. He has young children and decided the inherent risks of motorcycling were too much for a family man, but says he is counting the years till his kids graduate so he'll feel comfortable riding again. Jack runs an Outward Bound-type treatment center for young kids with substance abuse problems. Vivian, another friend from early recovery in Miami, joined us for lunch at a funky little noodle place on the main drag.

We had a wonderful time reconnecting. All three of us had come into recovery in the early eighties and now, with the benefit of hindsight, we understand how magical those days of early recovery are. We caught up and filled each other in on other friends from the early days and told both happy and sad tales of them. I guess we felt a bit like old veterans from some famous battle reuniting and reminiscing. After a few hours Jack had to run off for some family duties.

Although Vivian and I have known each other for nearly twenty-five years, we had never been particularly close. But within the past year, through a chance conversation while she was visiting Miami, we had discovered we were both grappling with similar personal issues that reached far back into our early lives, and she introduced me to another twelve-step fellowship that focused on that area—adult children of alcoholic/dysfunctional families. We continued talking over coffee until she had to leave for an appointment with a client. I had intended on getting back on the road right after lunch, but Vivian offered me her couch to crash on for the night, and we made plans to get together at her home later in the evening, grab a quick dinner, and hit a meeting.

With a couple hours to fill, I got my map from the bike and found a place under a tree in a small, triangularly-shaped park in the middle of town to plan my next day's route to Akron. I don't do much research or plan far ahead on these trips; I usually just pick the wiggliest road that's heading in the general direction I want to go and try to follow it the best I can, and modify on the fly if it doesn't feel right. I've seen some beautiful country, found some great roads, and always ended up where I wanted to be this way. It looked like heading north on I-26 and US Route 23 through the top of North Carolina into Tennessee, Virginia, and Kentucky would be a good way start out in the morning and would lead me to Southern Ohio where I could figure out the rest of the day's ride.

That settled, I studied the kids hanging out in the park. I recognized a younger version of myself in them from the year I'd spent hitchhiking around the country in 1980. They were hanging out, playing hacky sack, strumming guitars, and getting high. I even noticed one reading Kerouac. For the first time in decades I was approached and offered drugs. At lunch Jack had somewhat jokingly mentioned that these kids were future clients for some of the dozens of treatment centers around the area. It was an interesting reflection back to a time I'd lived before the drugs turned on me. I wish all of us well.

Vivian's home is nestled in a bamboo grove a couple miles out of town on a steep, twisty, narrow road that winds uphill above a swift mountain river. I found her place by the simple directions she gave me. I was a little nervous riding my heavily loaded bike around some of the turns that had loose gravel strewn across the road. My bike is a 2002 BMW R1150RT, a "sport touring" model. At six hundred fifty pounds before loaded with all my gear, it is the heaviest motorcycle I've owned. I bought it just two weeks before this trip and was getting used to it as I went along. It's a pure pleasure to ride at speed; it's fast and nimble with great weather protection, but it is a little top heavy at slow speeds and it's a bit tall for me.

I was worried about picking it up if I were to drop it, but I made it without a problem.

With all the treatment centers in the area, it's not surprising that Asheville has a large number of meetings among various fellowships. We discussed which fellowship we should go to and chose a meeting near her house, went out for coffee and dessert with a bunch of people from the meeting afterward, and returned to her place tired and ready for sleep around midnight.

Despite my dislike of interstates I must admit I-26 north of Asheville is a beautiful road. On Saturday morning it was mostly empty, which allowed me to relax and enjoy the scenery. I've always loved the way tall, brightly painted white steeples of churches were the only things that rose above the green trees in southern mountain towns. But now grey industrial-looking cell phone towers dwarf the pristine steeples of yesterday. I guess our need to constantly and immediately transmit many words now trumps the quiet spreading of "The Word." I also get a peaceful feeling from seeing the small cemeteries next to the churches with bright, colorful flowers sprouting from century-old headstones. There is a precious continuity and reverence for the importance of family in that. It's something many of us who grew up in busy urban environments never get exposed to.

That's one of the reasons I ride motorcycles—to learn a little of that way of life that still exists outside my busy city life.

At the Tennessee/Virginia state line, I-26 reverts back to its original form and number as US Route 23. Routes differ from interstates in that they will pass through towns and have cross streets and intersections with traffic lights instead of running past towns, requiring a traveler to exit at an interchange and get off the road to see what the area around the highway looks like. Some are still four-lane divided highways, but they are slower than the interstates, and they feel more connected to the people and the land near them.

I find them much less sterile too. In Kentucky, Route 23 has been designated the Country Music Highway. It's one of one hundred and fifty National Scenic Byways in the US, meaning it's a "destination road," a road worth traveling just to travel on. It was the first of two scenic byways I ended up riding that day. And one of a half-dozen I'd get to ride before returning home.

The guidebooks suggest spending two days exploring the 144 miles of the Country Music Highway—it's the area where the famous Hatfield and McCoy feud took place, and the place where Loretta Lynn, "the Coal Miner's Daughter," came from, as well as Billy Ray and Miley Cyrus. I passed through it in a little more than two hours, but enjoyed it as much as if I'd stopped at every point of interest along the way. I like being in motion. That's why I can cover long distances in a short time; long days in the saddle are as pleasurable for me as stopping at every historical marker is to a history buff. Sometimes I think I should slow down and notice the flowers more. But I wanted to get to Akron in the morning, so I pushed on.

I missed a road and got lost for a while after crossing into Southern Ohio. I wanted to head east and find my second scenic byway of the day, Ohio State Route 7, which runs parallel to the Ohio River. I ended up wandering through some industrial areas and having to stop and ask for directions before I found my way back to my intended route, which took me through rural farmland with lush green fields of corn lying between the twisty two-lane road and the river's edge on my right. I followed this road for about one hundred miles of relaxed riding, almost never losing sight of the historic river. I saw many bikes on the road out enjoying a late afternoon putt, and dozens of tugboats on the water pushing barges to destinations I will never know.

Eventually I needed to hit Interstate 77 for the northbound run up to Akron, but I resisted as long as possible. With about ten miles before SR-7 ran into I-77, I noticed Ohio State Road 339 out of the corner of my eye as I passed it by. It looked interesting, and my instincts told me it was worth turning around for. I'm glad I did.

So far, I'd started out on an interstate, gone to a US route, to a state route, and now I was on a state road. Each change dropped me down one level of what most people consider a better road. My rating system, and that of most riders, runs counter to conventional wisdom. This road was so twisty some of the curves had speed warnings as slow as fifteen and twenty miles per hour. I was in heaven. This is what's known as a "technical road." I couldn't just sit back in the saddle and go with the flow—well I guess I could have if I'd slowed down quite a bit—but I wanted to get the adrenaline flowing. For close to forty miles I had to calculate each curve, deciding on the correct entry speed and the best turn-in point. Sometimes I had to shift my weight off the seat and counter-weight the bike in order to get the best line through the turn, all the while staying hyper-alert for dirt or gravel that might have been spilled in the road from one of the many driveways leading off into cornfields alongside the road. This was an exciting road. That kind of road is one of the reasons I ride motorcycles.

Eventually SR-339 led me to I-77, and I headed north until I found a campground within a reasonable distance of Akron. I'd traveled more than seven hundred miles through some beautiful country and was real happy to climb into my tent at the end of a great day. Motorcycle jackets make terrible pillows, but I always seem to get a great night's sleep when that's all I have to rest my head on.

2

MANY OF MY FRIENDS who ride long distances have GPS units mounted on their bikes and will have programmed their entire trips before leaving their driveways. I guess you can call me a Luddite because I still prefer paper maps over technology. GPS probably would have kept me from getting lost and losing an hour at the Ohio border, but on the other hand, I might have missed that delightful ride along the river, and most certainly would have not stumbled on that devilishly twisty stretch that had me grinning in my helmet and riding on the sides of my tires. However, when it comes to navigating within a city, paper maps are a pain in the ass.

As I waited for the sun to dry the last bit of dew off my tent, I pulled out my phone, Googled Dr. Bob's home in Akron, hit a couple buttons, and let it plot a turn-by-turn route straight to the house. Talk about having the best of both worlds. I wrote the directions on an index card and slipped it into the clear map case that snaps onto the top of my tank bag. The house is open from noon to 3:00 p.m. every day, so I had time to stop at McDonald's for breakfast and take advantage of the free Wi-Fi there to catch up with email on my laptop before riding the last hundred miles into Akron.

On the ride into the city, I thought about my friend Rick who had told me about Dr. Bob's home. Rick and his son had gone through treatment together and only had a few months in recovery when they made the trip for the Founder's Day celebration in June 2005. Within a month of that visit, the disease of addiction separated Rick and his family from his young son forever. I hate the disease so much, but I'm equally grateful for the magic that grew out of those first meetings here in this industrial city in Ohio.

The streets in the historic neighborhood leading up to Dr. Bob's home are metaphorically perfect for this journey. This part of Akron is old enough that the streets are paved with real bricks— after traveling on smooth pavement for so long to get here, the last few miles are rough, and uncomfortable to travel over on my bike. I was glad when I arrived and it was time to stop. The house itself has, appropriately, twelve steps leading from the tree-lined street up to the front porch. And inside the house, it's nice and clean and comfortable, and everybody is welcoming and is there for the same purpose—to pay homage to the place where their true lives began.

Chad, the man who first greeted me when I walked in, introduced me to Kevin and Casey who had arrived just a few moments before me. Kevin is an Englishman from Dover who now lives in Hanoi, Viet Nam. Casey is from Akron. They first met eleven years prior on an army base in Japan when Kevin stumbled into his first twelve-step meeting. Kevin has remained in recovery; Casey's been struggling and hasn't, but they remain friends, and Casey says he's ready to give the program another try. Before I left a couple hours later I

HOME FOR SO MANY—DR. BOB'S HOUSE IN AKRON, OHIO

met a guy from San Diego, a group of four friends who drove down from Canada, and another dozen people from all over who share a reverence for this house equal to that of religious pilgrims visiting their most holy site.

Guiding us through the house, Chad told tales from the early days of AA and played a short film about the circumstances that brought Dr. Bob Smith and Bill Wilson together, and how the fellowship of recovery was born there through the discovery that the best way for someone to stay in recovery was to help someone else stay in recovery. That's what those two men discovered: We can't do it alone.

That first chance meeting eventually led to millions of meetings worldwide and more than four hundred variations of the twelve-step program where people recover lives that have been lost to drugs or alcoholism or compulsive gambling or obsessive overeating or unhealthy sexual behavior or even from the toxic effects of living with family members with the disease of addiction or other dysfunction.

Everyone who has been touched by what grew out of that first meeting in 1935 is a member of the fellowship of recovery and understands why I choked up when a stranger said, "Welcome home" at a house I'd never visited before.

Walking out to my bike after my visit, I remembered that ten years before Bill and Dr. Bob's meeting at that house, Bill and his wife Lois Wilson, founder of Al-Anon—the twelve-step "fellowship of relatives and friends of alcoholics who share their experience, strength, and hope in order to solve their common problems"*—had spent a year riding a Harley-Davidson sidecar rig from New York down to Florida and back. Lois kept a journal of that trip and wrote a book: *Diary of Two Motorcycle Hobos.* The book is out of print now, but copies occasionally come up on eBay or can be found from used book dealers. Lois writes about how Bill, while struggling to get

*Reprinted by permission of Al-Anon

PHOTOGRAPH COURTESY OF STEPPING STONES FOUNDATION

BILL AND LOIS WILSON WITH
THEIR HARLEY IN THE MID-1920S

sober, seemed happier than normal and wasn't drinking as much or as often as he had been before they began the ride. I guess, although motorcycles are not a magic cure-all, they have always been good vehicles for people on a journey to a better life.

My next stop was more than thirteen hundred miles to the west in Sturgis, South Dakota. I checked my map before heading south on I-77 and found a road, US Route 30, that looked promising. I stopped for gas and noticed a bunch of guys with their faces and bodies painted black and orange loading cases of beer into a minivan. I figured there was a football game somewhere and later rode past the Pro Football Hall of Fame, which was swarming with people sitting under tents on a low hill overlooking the freeway. Later I learned that was the day the Hall of Fame inducts new members, and there was an important football game somewhere nearby. Of course I thought those guys with the body paint were a little overboard in their enthusiasm, but when I noticed them looking at me strangely because I looked like a space alien on this mid-ninety degree day with my fancy Euro-Tech riding suit, heavy boots, silver full-face helmet with a black tinted face shield, and gauntlet style gloves, I just thought "To each his own," nodded and wished them a great day and continued on my way.

Route 30 used to be part of the historic Lincoln Highway, which was the first coast-to-coast road across the country. Today, in Ohio, it's a four-lane divided highway that passes through farmland, small towns, and a few medium-sized cities. It was a pleasant, easy ride without much traffic. About the only thing I had to worry about was the huge number of bugs that plastered my face shield; I had to stop every hour or so to clean them off so I could see the road in front of me. And the only thing I had to pay close attention to were the hundreds of motorcycles in the oncoming lanes. Every rider who came toward me on that Sunday afternoon waved. I must have spent half my time with my left hand up in the air waving back to my brothers and sisters in the wind. That's how we riders acknowledge the fellowship of the open road; we're so busy moving fast and far that we don't have time to stop and have meetings. So we wave.

Riding such a relaxing road, I was able to reflect on my own recovery and my using days.

I'm one of those who believe drugs saved my life. I was an awkward kid who grew up in an unhealthy home. I had attention-deficit/hyperactivity disorder (AD/HD) and dyslexia. School was impossible for me; I couldn't sit still, couldn't pay attention, was always talking out of turn, and couldn't concentrate on any task long enough to complete it. I was always getting in trouble and never understood why. I learned recently my parents were told I should have been in an accelerated learning program at school, but they didn't believe in coddling me and thought all I needed was to buckle down and behave. Today I would have received special attention, but in the early sixties I was looked at as having a discipline problem. My dad's form of discipline was pretty harsh; his tools were belittlement and sarcasm. He wasn't physically violent with me, but was verbally abusive. I grew up terrified of him, and my mother didn't have the capacity to understand my needs or give me the support I needed.

By fourth grade I'd had a brutal introduction to sex and, along with the constant condemnation and punishment from my parents and teachers, felt so defective and hopeless and was in so much emotional pain that I was suicidal and actually started to go through with it—but I couldn't even succeed at that. No one noticed my pain. I was a scared little kid who never learned a healthy way to interact with others. There was no single big thing that was wrong in my life; it was every little thing. I felt like I was being mauled to death by a pack of Chihuahuas. All I could do was withdraw from the world.

I began to occasionally sneak alcohol whenever I could while still in elementary school and started using drugs in junior high. By my first year in high school (emphasis on the "high"), I was a daily user and didn't quit till I was twenty-seven years old.

The drugs not only allowed me to function through my pain, they gave me a social life, helped me get laid, and eventually became a part-time occupation. I had a lot of fun for a lot of years. But, as it happens to everyone who depends on substances to cope with day-to-day living, they eventually turned on me and I became a prisoner of my addiction.

I understand now why using chemicals to cope with emotional pain backfires. It's like an animal with a physical injury: If a dog breaks his leg, you can't give him pain medication because he'll forget he's hurt and continue walking on the wounded leg, causing more damage. People who self-medicate to cover up emotional injuries and try to continue to function as if nothing were wrong end up causing deeper psychological damage to themselves. But in order to survive my childhood, I had to numb myself from my feelings just to stay alive. Drugs helped me until they started to kill me. I ended up crawling into a twelve-step program.

When I first found recovery my life improved immediately. First I got healthy, and then my job and financial situation improved. I met my wife in the rooms—we've been together since 1985. I went back to school, got a degree, and began a career. I've been able to ride motorcycles all across the country numerous times, and I've ridden on a number of racetracks including Daytona.

My life got good.

But I always had that wounded little boy living inside me and never truly felt like I belonged in the world. Eventually his wounds festered and began to infect me, and I started losing the ability to function. My world began to unravel and my momentum waned. I'd had some fantastic luck in the early years of a new career. I had the talent to do good work, but lost the ability to handle the social aspects of the job and began to falter. Then my little sister passed away, and my family didn't give me the opportunity to attend her funeral. I realized my family just didn't understand my need to be at my sister's service, and from that I began to realize they had never known how to give me what I needed when I was a child, and all those old hurts I'd buried years ago resurfaced.

I started seeing a therapist who diagnosed me with depression and prescribed antidepressants—they didn't help.

A program at the psych department of a local university diagnosed me with post-traumatic stress disorder from my childhood—but they didn't have a solution to my problem other than trying to teach me how to learn to ignore the feelings and get on with my life. That's what I'd been trying to do all along and it didn't work anymore.

I tried to talk about those old issues with my family, but they weren't able to go there and we haven't spoken in years now.

The Chihuahuas were closing in, and I felt like I was being pulled down into a dark, ugly vortex that would suck me into an emptiness so deep I'd never be able to climb out into sunshine again. This was all internal. All this time on the surface everything seemed normal. I continued to work; I was involved with volunteer activities in the community; I stayed clean and went to meetings and kept my life together as best I could. But I was dying on the inside. This was a bottom of another sort, similar to how I'd felt at the end of my using, but different because the solution was elusive. It wasn't as clear as giving up drugs and alcohol.

About the only relief I got was when I'd head out on my motorcycle—somehow my demons never learned to ride.

Eventually my friend Vivian told me about another fellowship that had a few new meetings in Miami and suggested I check it out. I walked into my first meeting and knew I was home. People were talking about growing up in abusive, dysfunctional homes, and the Twelve Steps were adapted to recover from the damage of those upbringings. When I went to my very first meeting in 1983 someone told me, "You never have to use drugs again." I believed him, and I haven't. I felt the same relief at this meeting. I was told, "If you can handle what comes up at these meetings, your life will change." I knew I'd found a place where I could share about how I felt with people who understood and had been there. They could help me where therapists, university programs, and medications couldn't. I had found a new fellowship for the next stage of my recovery.

The journey of recovery is different for everyone. For some it's like an apple: they bite through the skin into the fruit, get nourishment, and get healthy. For others it's like an avocado: they have to cut it open, throw away the pit, and eat the meat from inside the skin to grow strong. For me it's an onion; I have to keep pulling off layers and shedding tears to get to the core. Those tears are the water that nourishes my true self and gives me the strength to grow and branch out and blossom.

This motorcycle trip was part of my journey. Besides having a fun ride across the continent looking for adventure, twisty roads, new country, and visiting with six hundred thousand of my closest friends in Sturgis, I wanted free time to think. There is nothing like stuffing your head inside a motorcycle helmet for ten hours a day, day after day, to work things out. Also, I hoped to be able to find time to ride out to my hometown of Seattle and look for hints I could use on my newfound recovery, and maybe even stop in and see my parents in Oregon, whom I hadn't spoken to in six years.

I crossed from Ohio into Indiana as evening came on. I had an appointment in a few hours and had to find a place to stop. The new fellowship I'd found had a step meeting on Sunday nights. That meeting had become so important to me that the thought of missing it almost kept me from taking this trip. I'd mentioned this to someone in the group, and he talked it over with a few other members; they decided to put a phone on speaker and pass it around the room during the meeting so I could call in from wherever I was on the road and attend through the wonder of modern communication.

At 7:00 p.m. (EST), I found a grassy spot next to a dumpster behind a Steak 'n Shake in Fort Wayne, Indiana and phoned in to my meeting.

I don't have the words to explain what that did for me. To have a group of people share my journey out of that black despair I'd been living, to know they understand my need, and to have them make such an effort to keep me connected, even from halfway across the country, is indescribable.

That's fellowship. Bill W and Dr. Bob would have been proud.

3

I'M A NEWS JUNKIE. At home I read a couple different papers every day and follow numerous websites to keep up with current events, but when I'm out on the road I try to ignore all that. I figure the world will survive without me monitoring it, and if it is about to end, I'd rather remain ignorant so it doesn't ruin my ride. All the news I need I can get from the Weather Channel.

Route 30 runs below the southern point of Lake Michigan, where I had the option of staying on 30; jumping up to Interstate 90 and riding directly to South Dakota on the super slab through Illinois, Wisconsin, and Minnesota; or heading due west on Interstate 80 through Illinois, partway into Iowa, then working my way north on back roads to Sturgis. Whatever route I choose, the Weather Channel informed me that I would probably get real wet. There was a huge storm with strong winds blowing across the Dakotas and the upper Midwest, with heavy flooding in Iowa from thunderstorms that seemed to have set up residence over the state for the summer.

I decided to prepare for the worst, hope for the best, and depend on the weather apps on my phone for last-minute routing decisions.

My bike has two factory saddlebags and a top case behind the passenger seat. I keep my clothes and toiletries in the right-side bag, and my rain gear, a spare face shield, a pair of shoes, and a quart of oil on the left side. The top case holds all my electronics— laptop, camera equipment, four different chargers and cords to keep the electricity in those things, a large flashlight, and my notebooks and reading material. My camping gear goes into a once-waterproof duffle bag strapped onto the passenger seat. And I have a tank bag, which sits on the gas tank in front of me, where I keep things I want easy access to such as snacks, maps, my phone, spare gloves, sunglasses, a small notebook for jotting down thoughts, a cable for locking my helmet to the bike, a plastic 35mm film canister with change for tolls, a mini flashlight, spare earplugs, a tire pressure gauge, and other small items.

BMW luggage is good quality, and I wasn't worried about anything in there getting wet. I wrapped my tent, sleeping bag, and mattress into plastic garbage bags and repacked them into the duffle; all the stuff from my tank bag went into resealable plastic bags. I folded my map into a plastic case that snaps onto the top of the tank bag, and I hoped it would stay dry in there.

It was hot and humid and the sky hung low and dark above the land as I loaded the bike in the morning at the cheap motel where I'd spent the night in Indiana. It wasn't raining yet so I compromised on rain gear. My riding suit is a four-part deal: a jacket-and-pants set with an abrasion-resistant mesh outer shell made of Cordura that has plastic armor sewn into the back and over the knees, elbows, shoulders, and hips in case I end up sliding down the road sometime without the bike between me and the asphalt. A wind and waterproof inner liner zips and snaps inside the shells to makes it an all-weather kit. My boots are waterproof, and I have a pair of waterproof over-gloves in my tank bag that I can pull on over my regular vented riding gloves. I used the pant liners but kept the jacket's liner in the saddle bag as I pulled out of the parking lot. I could always stop and get the jacket liner on quickly, but pulling off the pants shell to climb into those liners on the side of the road could be a problem.

At home around town, I'm a Levis and T-shirt rider, but on trips like this, where I'm averaging five to six hundred miles per day, day after day, proper riding gear adds a lot to my comfort level. My outfit is a RUKKA suit from Finland, and it's about as high-tech as is possible to find. It is black with lots of bright, colorful labeling and reflective piping; its Euro-styling is the complete opposite of my fashion sense, and I'm self-conscious whenever I'm wearing it off the bike. Motorcycling is an equipment sport—the better the equipment, the more enjoyable the activity, so I tolerate the stares. I've stayed dry in this suit riding through rainstorms that would make Noah run for cover. It's kept me as comfortable as can be without air conditioning on summer rides with temperatures up to 115 degrees, and, with a set of electric-heated underwear, warm on winter rides when it's been down below freezing. It cost more than the first brand-new motorcycle I bought in 1975, but it's proven worth every penny. Leather and denim fit the biker image better, but modern gear allows me to be prepared for a wide range of conditions and feel safe with a minimum of stuff to pack.

Route 30 started rural as I headed out from my motel, but became urban as I neared the Indiana/Illinois state line. I crawled through heavy traffic past strip malls, car dealerships, and all the other congestion modern living requires. Stuck at traffic lights for two or three changes before I could move on to the next, I decided the interstate might be a better choice, and then it started to rain. I stopped at an open-early hot dog joint for breakfast, donned the jacket liner, and checked the weather radar on my phone. It looked completely ugly to the north, but there were some gaps in the systems to the west so I hopped on I-80 in Joliet, Illinois and aimed for Iowa surrounded by big rigs heading out of Chicago for who knows where with their Monday morning loads.

With time the traffic thinned out and the rain let up. I crossed the Mississippi River into Iowa and rode out from under the overcast into a clear blue sky. It got brutally hot and I needed to stop and shed the rain liners; I saw a sign advertising "Iowa 80—The World's Largest Truck Stop" up ahead at the town of Walcott and figured to stop there until I spotted it from the highway. It's huge. It must cover ten to fifteen acres; there are more fuel pumps out front than candles on the altar at a Catholic mass. Later I learned this travel plaza has multiple restaurants, a movie theater, a barbershop, a dentist office, a museum, a pet wash, and even an embroidery center. I would have gotten lost on my little bike amongst all the cars, trucks, and tourists.

Down the road I pulled into a rest area and removed the extra layer of clothing in the air-conditioned restroom. Coming back to my bike, I met a young kid, freshly graduated from college, who was parked next to me on his brand-new Yamaha with a half-dozen duffle bags strapped on the passenger seat behind him. Everything he had was new and clean and shiny; his fluorescent-yellow one-piece riding suit even still had creases in it. He was riding from Virginia to Alaska. I didn't ask, but I got the impression his trip was a graduation present from his family. He told me he had the entire trip mapped out on his GPS; he knew where he'd be camping each night, where to get his bike serviced, and what time he'd get to Seattle to catch the ferry up the inland passage to Alaska. I thought of my friend Doug, who did a long motorcycle trip when he graduated from college in the early nineties. He rode whatever bike he had at the time, and the only new thing he carried was a current list of each city's helpline numbers so he could find meetings along the way.

DOUG

I grew up on two wheels, though they were never my own because my parents wouldn't allow it. I rode homemade mini bikes in elementary school and a Yamaha YZ-80 in junior high. I bought my first bike, if you can call it that, at fifteen: a Puch moped (I kept it in a friend's yard so my mom wouldn't know). It was the kind you start by pedaling as fast as you can then yanking on a starter clutch. Of course it was souped up a bit. It topped out at a whopping forty miles per hour downhill. It wasn't fast, but it was too fast for this fifteen-year-old punk on dope.

I must have wrecked that thing every other week. One night I decided to go get more beer, and as I was getting on the moped, my mother's poodle Bambino gave me that forlorn "I wanna go" look. It went pretty smoothly at first, until Bambino started wriggling around. As I was laying the moped down, I was just sober enough to throw the little furball into the soft grassy swale. Another night, I wiped out in my own driveway. I learned that night why bikers don't wear flip flops. I spent the next month riding around with a pair of crutches sticking off the book rack like a pair of aluminum wings. I knew that drinking and driving a two-wheeled motorized vehicle was dangerous. I wasn't stupid. My best thinking was that at night I would put the moped keys in my mother's nightstand. However, that never worked. I would just end up crawling past my sleeping parents like a stoned ninja and hitting the road.

DOUG ON HIS GRADUATION RIDE IN THE EARLY NINETIES

The end of my first "bike" came one night, when, like so many other nights, I ran out of drugs sometime around 2 a.m. I hopped on my Puch scooter and took off for my dealer's apartment. She wasn't there, but instead of going straight home, I stopped at a new housing complex near my house to steal a flag (I was strictly small time).

Unfortunately, the flag was screwed to a ten-foot pipe. Instead of giving up my master plan, I pulled the whole pole out of the ground and headed for home. Once again things started out just fine, but my luck ran out when I had to turn onto my street. The pole hit the front tire and wouldn't let it turn. Being too drunk to realize I could let go of the pole, I ended up only turning forty-five degrees, not the ninety required to complete the turn. As you can probably guess, there was a tree on the corner. When I came to, the moped was still running, and I was still holding the flagpole. I picked up the moped and limped the last block to my house. I walked through my house banging that pole against doors, walls, and lamps. As I stumbled into my bedroom and passed out, I dropped the blood-soaked flag and pole.

The next day I called my mother at work and told her I had been in an accident. Her only question was, "Were you drinking?" "Yes," I said. "Well, you're on your own." When the doctor called her a couple of hours later, she softened up a bit.

Fast forward five years, I had given up drinking and drugging, but not riding. I had about three years in recovery and was living in Los Angeles and going to college. I lived in the dorms and went to meetings in Venice, Santa Monica, and Hollywood. Usually I took the bus to meetings, but sometimes I borrowed a buddy's Honda Elite 50 if he wasn't using it—not very cool, but perfect for college. There was a hot biker chick who rode a Sportster at one of my regular meetings. Every week after the meeting, I would ask her if she wanted to go for a ride. I'd say, "We've got to stay on the city streets because it's illegal for me go on the freeway." For some reason I never got anywhere with that woman.

When I was close to graduation, I started to plan the obligatory post-college European trip—the one where you buy that train pass and travel around with nothing but a backpack. However, under the category of "Life is what happens while you're busy making other plans," the first Gulf War broke out. Travel advisories and rumors of Americans being targeted put a crimp in my trip plans. Not being one to relish the thought of being targeted, I began looking for options. I certainly didn't want to get a job.

Voila! A cross-country motorcycle trip—the other great American journey.

By this time I was riding a 1981 Honda CB900c for a couple of years, but I had never taken a trip on it or any other motorcycle. As I packed up the back of the bike with what I thought was the bare minimum, I realized I had way too much stuff. I ended up leaving clothes and gear in an empty Santa Monica apartment, and my bike still looked like Fred Sanford's truck on the seventies sitcom *Sanford and Son*. Armed with two lists, the first a list of twelve-step helplines across the US and the second a list of all fifty states' helmet laws, I hit the road. Traveling north on the Pacific Coast Highway that first day, I lost my sleeping bag off the back of the bike.

My first stop was Santa Barbara, California, and I stayed with my sister's best friend. The next night I camped on a secluded and incredibly beautiful beach. The wind just about shredded my tent. On day three, I got to Santa

Cruz and checked into a youth hostel. Once settled in, I cruised through the University of California, Santa Cruz and went to a meeting. Afterward, I went down to the beach with a couple of other recovering addicts to see a kite festival. The next day was July fourth, and the friends I had made at the meeting invited me to hang around for the parade and fireworks, but I was already obsessed with hitting the road. I had to get the wind in my face.

Continuing north up the coast, I crossed into Oregon on day six. I went to a meeting in a town called Bandon and hung out with a guy who had just celebrated three years in recovery and was bicycling south. Wow, and I thought I was roughing it. When I asked him how to lighten my load, he asked me how many pairs of pants I had. When I proudly answered, "Only two," he asked, "Why do you need two?" I couldn't think of a reason.

The next meeting I went to was in Corvalis, Oregon. At that meeting I befriended a teenage runaway who was trying to stay clean. I was staying with my brother, who was a little unsure about this street urchin I had brought into his house to provide with a safe place to sleep, but he agreed to it. In the morning after the three of us had breakfast, I bought and installed a fairing onto the bike to lessen the wind blast because I was getting tendonitis in my shoulder.

I dropped my new friend off at a clubhouse to wait for the lunchtime meeting and I headed out. As I continued north, I hit meetings in Spokane and Seattle, Washington. Turning east from the coast, the riding days became longer and the meetings sparser. The only meeting I went to between Seattle and Rapid City, South Dakota was in Jackson Hole, Wyoming.

When I pulled into Rapid City on day twenty-eight, I had a couple of days to kill before my girlfriend, Cindy, flew in for the fifty-first Black Hills Rally, so I tuned up the bike, washed clothes, poked around the Badlands, and went to a couple of meetings. In Sturgis, the AA clubhouse was buzzing with the planning of the next day's clean and sober poker run.

In the morning, I woke up early to head to Sturgis and took along one of the European girls staying at the youth hostel. My rider didn't understand the whole recovery aspect of it, but she was just as excited as I was about the ride. The only other time I had joined in on such a large ride was the Love Ride in Los Angeles, but that was just a bunch of individuals riding in the same direction. This was going to be different. This was a ride with around two hundred of my brothers and sisters. And it was everything I expected it to be. I purposely positioned myself in the middle of the pack. I loved the idea of seeing nothing but bikes as far ahead and as far behind as the eye could see. At every stop, along with poker cards and refreshments, there was recovery. Every stranger was a friend. You didn't just compliment someone on their bike; you gave him or her a hug too. By the end of the day, I had more offers of places to stay throughout the rest of my trip than I could have possibly needed.

When Cindy got in the next day, I was charged and ready to go. We spelunked a couple of caves, rode to Mount Rushmore and Devils Tower, and swam in as many cool streams as we could find. We spent the night in a teepee in the Badlands, and spent a couple of days just hanging out in Sturgis and Deadwood. By the time I said goodbye and put Cindy back on the plane to LA, I was once again ready to ride.

I was only about a third of the way through my trip. For the next two months, I rode east, then south, and finally back west. I slept in my tent, in hostels, with friends and family, and occasionally under bridges. I hit meetings in Madison, Milwaukee, Chicago, Allentown, Asheville, Miami, Key West, San Antonio, and other small towns that I can't recall the names of. After ninety-three days and over twelve thousand miles, I got back to LA safe and sound and moved in with my sponsor. No crashes or major break downs, and the only ticket I got was on day one in LA for jaywalking back to my bike from an ATM.

That was eighteen years ago now, and I'm still going to meetings. But because of my children, I've traded in my bikes for boats. Truth be told, I don't miss the city riding one bit. It's the open road that I still dream of. I'm already looking forward to when I can hit the road again on two wheels and go to as many meetings in as many places as I can.

My mother had been raised in Iowa, and we used to drive out to visit in the family station wagon when I was a kid. I decided to see if I could find her hometown. The last time we were there was 1968; I was twelve and only have a faint memory of the trip. I remembered there was a religious shrine in her town. A little Googling on my phone, and I found the Grotto of the Redemption in the town of West Bend, Iowa.

It was sort of on my way. The late afternoon sky was beginning to get dark, so I checked the weather and found it was clear in that direction. I bailed from the interstate at Iowa City and began weaving and wandering on a series of state and county roads heading northwest. Riding through Iowa this way was fun. The roads were

THE GROTTO OF THE REDEMPTION IN WEST BEND, IOWA

mostly straight and flat with sharp ninety-degree turns. I guess road engineers in farm country defer to the property lines of large farms so that the land seems to be divided into square, city-type blocks that have been stretched out to giant-sized proportions and stripped of all buildings except for farmhouses with big barns out back alongside tall silos and well-maintained outbuildings.

Occasionally I'd see an old, weather-beaten, two-story house in the middle of a field, leaning precariously to one side and looking like it was still standing only out of a century-old habit. Corn would be growing up to within a tractor's tire-width of its walls, and no driveway or road led to its sagging pouch. I imagine it was the original homesteader's house of a family farm and was left standing for the same reason headstones in southern states warrant fresh flowers from successive generations who may have never known the inhabitants they were honoring.

I rolled into West Bend just before dark; I needed gas and had no idea where I'd spend the night. With an official population of 763 and a landmass of less than one square mile carved out of the cornfields that surround it on all sides, it's not exactly a thriving metropolis and I had no idea if anything would be open that late. I found a place for gas on the road leading into town and bought a few things that would substitute for dinner in case I didn't find a place to eat.

I only had a vague memory of the Grotto. There wasn't any good reason it should have stuck in my head all these years, but I've never forgotten it. It was built by a German-born Catholic priest to fulfill a promise made to the Virgin Mary if she'd answer his prayer to spare his life from a near-fatal illness. Under his direction, without formal plans, millions and millions of rocks, stones, and precious gems have been individually cemented in place by him and a team of volunteers to build a monument to God. It fills a complete city block, with nine sections depicting different stages in the life of Jesus. It would have been either the most wonderful or the most terrifying place to trip—no in-between.

When later researching the Grotto, I discovered some riders from local twelve-step programs have an annual "Blessing of the Bikes" there in the spring when the weather begins clearing before the summer riding season. I spoke on the phone with one of the organizers, who told me they get a good turnout every year with riders coming in from all over Iowa and neighboring states.

The Grotto was closed for the night, but there is a campground in a field across the street complete with hot showers and Wi-Fi. My question about where to spend the night was answered; I planned on touring the Grotto in the morning before making a final push through to Sturgis.

After my shower, a swarm of mosquitoes chased me into my tent before I was ready for sleep. The walls of my tent are mostly fine netting meant to keep mosquitoes and other bugs out while letting a breeze flow freely through. It has a waterproof rainfly for when the weather gets cold or wet, or for when I want privacy. There weren't many others at the Grotto's campground, so I left the fly off so I could watch the moon rise and look at the night sky, and I laid awake for a long time thinking about what I knew of my mother's life here in Iowa.

PHOTOGRAPH COURTESY OF THE GROTTO OF REDEMPTION

BLESSING OF THE BIKES AT THE GROTTO

She had been taken away from her mother when she was only three and brought to Iowa from California to be raised by an aunt and uncle who never fully adopted her as one of their own. When she turned eighteen she moved back to the West Coast to be with her mother, which turned out to be a disaster. I suppose she was looking for a love and nurturing that she never felt with her Iowa family, but she didn't get it. My grandmother was a hard woman who had had a hard life. She wasn't the nurturing type, and she and my mother had a huge falling out soon after they'd reunited. I'm sure my mom felt betrayed and abandoned; I don't know what my grandmother felt, but they didn't speak for many years, until I was born.

In later years my grandmother would tell me how abusive her mother had been to her. She'd left her home in Montana when she was sixteen and got a job as a truck driver in California—pretty rough stuff for a young girl in the 1920s. She got married and pregnant with my mother, but divorced before my mother was born. My mother never knew her father.

Family dysfunction is a generational thing. It gets refined and takes different forms as it's passed on. My grandmother didn't treat my mother the way she'd been treated, and my mother certainly treated me differently than she'd been raised. But the underlying damage filters down from parent to child. I didn't suffer the abuse of my grandmother or the abandonment of my mother, but my early life had been equally damaged in its own unique way. I've suffered from that all my life, but I have tools today, through the Twelve Steps, to work past the harm. My mom and grandma never had that opportunity.

I thought about my father too. He was raised on a farm in a small town in central Canada. I don't know much of his life; he was pretty closed about personal thoughts and feelings, but he did drop a few hints that he didn't have a happy childhood. I don't know any details about why, but he was a very angry man. He didn't let it out much; in fact, everyone who knows him praises his calmness and patience and goodness. The only time his anger escaped was toward me, and he could be cruel and cutting. I felt like he hated me; I was scared of him. Maybe there's some Freudian explanation that applies—I don't know and it doesn't really matter at this point. I'm working on myself, not on him.

A long train rumbled by on tracks I hadn't noticed on the far side of the campground. The sound was comforting, though unfamiliar in its closeness, and the cadence of rolling steel against track lulled me off to sleep.

4

I WOKE TO THE sound of loud thunder. In the distance a lightning storm kept me entertained until a layer of clouds began blowing in, obscuring my view; soon I smelt rain in the air so I scrambled out of the tent and pulled the rainfly into place. I fell back asleep before the rain started to fall, but when I did awake with the coming of first light, I was in a full-blown deluge. I was glad I'd taken the time to find the highest spot of ground to set my tent on, as I was sure water would be pooling in the low areas—Boy Scout training comes in handy again.

When the storm abated, I got up, packed, and rolled out without waiting for the Grotto to open. Rain was falling again by the time I got out of town and the roads were soaked. Many of the cornfields were partially flooded, and I could see a lot of crops had been wiped out by the recent rains. I headed north on Iowa Highway 15, which would take me to US Route 18 where I'd start heading west.

Highway 15 sort of stair-steps its way north and to the east a bit; I'd ride north for a few miles, then have to take one of those ninety-degree right turns, go east for a while, then turn north again. I'd repeated this a number of times and then missed a turn. Something distracted me and I looked up to see a stop sign right in front of me. I grabbed for my brakes and checked for traffic on the cross road—it was clear so I just ran the stop and continued north. My bike has ABS and I'm sure I could have stopped safely, even on the wet road, but, with no traffic coming, it was easier to roll through. Apparently that was one of those turns I should have taken to stay on Highway 15, since the road markers indicated I was on a county road. "No problem," I thought. The road number was followed by the letter "N," so I assumed, despite the fact that this road had some twists and turns on it, I was still headed north.

After an hour or so the rain let up and the morning sun burned through the clouds—on my left. I'd somehow gotten turned around and was headed south even though the road signs still had that reassuring "N" on them. I stopped, but couldn't locate myself on my map, and my phone was out of range so I couldn't find my way using its mapping program. Eventually I found a road where I could put the sun behind my back. I turned onto a narrow county road and headed west looking for larger roads.

I was aggravated by getting lost; I was hungry; and I was uncomfortably hot wearing all my raingear under the full sun, which caused me to become frustrated and impatient. I wasn't enjoying the ride. I've ridden enough to realize it's not safe to ride when it's not fun. When I get in that frazzled state of mind it's time to stop and take care of myself.

Breakfast at a roadside restaurant and some pleasant banter with the friendly waitress brought me back to myself. I got out of the raingear and picked up a state map, figured out where I was and how to get to where I wanted to be, and was good to go again.

I found US Route 18—a nice road through Northern Iowa with plenty of curves and gentle hills—and headed west toward Sturgis. The weather kept alternating between brutal heat and drenching thunderstorms. I left the raingear off to take advantage of the coolness from the rain. Besides, I'd dry out within a few miles after each storm, and the time lost putting it on and taking it off again would have annoyed me more than getting wet did.

My initial plan was to stay on Route 18 to the Black Hills National Forest on the western edge of South Dakota then head up to Sturgis, but by the time I got to the Iowa/South Dakota border, I decided to jump up to Interstate 90 at Sioux Falls and just make time.

It's around four hundred long miles across the state on I-90. The road is straight and flat without much to look at other than open prairie until nearing the Black Hills. My bike gets around three hundred miles from a tank of gas so I could have made it with only one fill-up, but I found myself stopping at truck stops almost every hour or so just to break the monotony, clean dead bugs off my face shield, get out of the heat for a few moments, and guzzle a bottle of water.

As I got closer to Sturgis, I began to see small groups, four or five members each, of a motorcycle club wearing their colors and hanging out in the shade in front of the buildings at each stop. I suppose this was a welcoming committee of sorts, whether to greet their own brothers or to make a show of presence to other clubs, I don't know. But I do know that many riders are intimidated by one-percenter motorcycle clubs, and the parking spots next to their bikes were usually empty. My experience with guys in clubs is that they are normally respectful to "civilians." I'd pull into a space near their Harleys—always right next to the front entrance—and almost every time would get a friendly nod that sometimes led into long conversations that started out with a question about my bug-splattered, German-built motorcycle.

By the time I got to Rapid City there were thousands of motorcycles on the road heading in every direction; we outnumbered cars and trucks by a huge margin, and it felt good to be among a two-wheeled majority. I didn't know where I was going, so I just followed the flow on the highway and ended up on Junction Avenue, one of the main drags leading into Sturgis. I hadn't made any plans and didn't have any idea where I was going to stay. I knew there were plenty of campgrounds, some of them right on the grounds of multi-acre bars that earn a year's worth of profit during the weeks around the rally, but I wasn't excited about staying at "Party Central," and hoped to find something a little less hectic.

A guy on an old Ironhead Sportster pulled up next to me in the crawling parade of overheating motorcycles going into town—later I discovered this was the route that led to where Bob Dylan was playing that night—and asked me if I had a place to stay yet. Over the roar of open pipes, he told me a guy on the next block up the street had room in his backyard for a couple more tents. He said he'd been staying there for years and I'd be welcome to camp there also. He pointed to the house and I could see a bunch of guys sitting in the front yard on lawn chairs, drinking beer, and watching the bikes roll past.

I thanked him for his hospitality, but decided to look for something a little quieter and friendlier to my fellowship and kept going. A friend in Miami named Bean're had told me about a church in town where a local twelve-step fellowship holds meetings every three hours each day of the rally and hosts a breakfast every morning. I figured I'd find it and ask around there about a place to camp.

After my high-speed push across South Dakota, my bike was starting to get hot in the ninety-five-degree, stop-and-go crawl into Sturgis. I pulled onto a side street and found a shady spot to let the bike cool. I got my phone out to see if I could figure out where the church Bean're told me about was. The only thing I remembered was that it had a red door.

Looking up from my phone while waiting for Google to connect, I noticed a church across the street from my resting spot with a bunch of canopies, picnic tables, and coolers out front—and a red door. A sign with a triangle inside of a circle let me know I'd found home base. I walked over and hung out, talking to riders from all over the country and eventually ran into another rider from Florida; turns out we had some mutual friends in Miami and he offered to introduce me to Wayne and Carolyn, a couple with a ranch outside Sturgis who host a campout on their property for "friends of Bill W" every year during the rally.

THE CHURCH WITH THE RED DOOR IN STURGIS

WAYNE AND CAROLYN

This is our story of how we started our Friends of Bill W camp in Sturgis, South Dakota—what it was like, what happened, what it is now.

I was born in Bear Butte, South Dakota, near the city of Sturgis. As a kid I looked forward to the motorcycle rally every year. As teenagers, my sister Colleen and I would ask the guys who came to town for the rally to take us for rides around town and out through the Black Hills. Back then the rally wasn't anything like it is today.

Hitching rides and partying with the bikers was fun, but that's about as far as I got into the biker scene. I never learned how to ride and didn't have any interest in motorcycles. My passion was riding and exploring the backcountry on horses and mules.

I met my husband Wayne and we moved to Arizona in the late sixties. Wayne didn't drink, but I did. Eventually, like so many of us, my drinking got out of hand and I ended up finding recovery in a twelve-step program. My recovery date is November 15, 1979.

Wayne loved me and supported me while I was in active addiction and continued to support me and love me in my early recovery, but he didn't understand the compulsion to drink or why it was so important for me to continue to go to meetings. He began to attend meetings of another twelve-step program for family members of addicts, and we have been sharing recovery for thirty-one of the forty-two years we've been married now.

In 1999 we retired and returned to the Black Hills. We built a ranch along the highway a couple miles outside Sturgis. That first year, Jordan, a friend from my home group, the Cactus Capers, rode his bike to the rally from Arizona and set up his tent in our yard. The next year he came back with a couple other guys from the group in Arizona, the next a few more came, then those guys came back the following year with some more of their friends, and now we are sharing our experience, strength, hope, and recovery with biker friends from all over the country and the world. And we get to meet a few new people and make new friends every year too.

Now I ride once a year on the annual Serenity Ride through the Black Hills that my local clubhouse sponsors. We ride from Sturgis and stop for lunch and a meeting near Mount Rushmore. We keep the ride down to three hundred bikes and have to turn away riders who didn't register in time every year.

When we first moved back to South Dakota, we didn't know if we would find meetings or a group we'd be comfortable with. We had a longing for our program in Arizona, but God has blessed us by delivering recovery right to our front door. This is a program of miracles.

A big, grizzled chopper pilot named Rick—who claims his long, salt-and-pepper hair is "not grey, it's chrome" and jokes that he's so old school, he's pre-school—explained to me the Black Hills are one of earth's great "power centers," where mysterious forces, ancient spirits, and the earth's energy itself all come to the surface to coalesce and become accessible to those seeking wisdom and knowledge. I wondered if Rick hadn't done one too many hits of acid back in his day, but whatever it was that Rick was talking about, there was a deep, warm, infectious energy at Wayne and Carolyn's place that I couldn't help but feel. Whether the magic comes from the land or from the people I don't know. I do know that Carolyn and Wayne facilitate something rare and special where the best of both the motorcycling and recovery fellowships meld into a roaring, high-octane, spiritual celebration of recovery, independence, and community. I'm grateful and feel fortunate to be a part of it.

RICK

Motorcycles and recovery, what do they have in common? Simple…FREEDOM. That's what it's all about, baby! Since day one it has been mankind's quest. Our country and every other democracy was founded on that premise. "Set my people free," "Let my people go," "Give me liberty or give me death." It don't take a rocket scientist to figure that one out.

I first got into motorcycles for that very reason. To get out of the constraints of a cage and feel the wind in my face and hair. To be a part of nature, exposed to the elements, good or bad. With that comes a cost. Personally, starting at the bottom and working up through my mangled body, I have had three broken toes, two shattered ankles, fifty stitches in my right leg, torn ligaments in both knees, three cracked ribs, bullet holes clean through me (a biker lifestyle kinda thing, doncha know), my nose, forehead, and scalp torn off, and multiple concussions (they say it causes dain brammage, but I don't think it has affected me none, yuk-yuk).

And my wife is paralyzed from the waist down from a scooter wreck down in Austin, Texas thirty years ago, but she still rides a hand controlled '77 Shovelhead Trike. God love her.

RICK CELEBRATING LIFE ON HIS GOOD TIMES CHARLEY BIKE

We have paid our dues big time but cannot give up riding. It's what I live for—my essence and my being.

I thought I had the freedom to do whatever I wanted—to drink as much as I could, to do any drugs that came along, and to ride hell-bent afterward. Man, that was freedom.

Of course the law had other ideas on that subject. I've got four driving while intoxicated charges under my belt and on my record. But those scooters were always running the best they ever did when I was whacked out of my gourd!

When I wasn't riding, I was wrenching on them getting even more blitzed. Falling down, stereo wide open, puking drunk. You'd better not bother me; I don't care who you are—wife, kids, whatever. If you didn't share in my oblivion you didn't matter. And I'd let you know it with a tirade of obscenities and violence. I was one mean son of a gun!

Then when morning came around all too soon it was off to work, still drunk, choking down Pepto-Bismol, aspirin, etc. to kill the pain and sickness. Tearing everyone around me a new asshole because I was the only one who had it figured out and they were all inferior. I hated everyone and everything. If you made more money than me you were a f**king yuppie; if you had less money than me you were a curb worm. If you were a religious person you were weak; if you weren't you were lost. Everyone was an idiot, and all other races were subhuman and open to every slanderous, disgusting joke I could come up with. Even other bikers were below my standards of what a true biker was, which I thought I and I alone exemplified.

But who I really hated was myself, although I wouldn't recognize or admit it. So I stewed in my hatred and soothed myself with my alcohol and drugs. I was alone in my fantasy. It was a vicious cycle of getting wasted one day, licking my wounds the next, and then doing it all over again, forgetting all the pain I had caused myself and everyone around me.

Man that was freedom. What I didn't know was how imprisoned I was by my actions.

I was in a hellhole of my own making. I had slammed the cell door shut on myself, my soul, and the beauty of life. I had been telling people how I was going to kill my wife and kids, burn down the house, and kill myself. My daughter overheard me and my whole family went to bed wondering if it would be their last night alive when I came stumbling in from the shop at three in the morning, insane from intoxication.

They arranged an intervention one evening when I came home from work still hungover from the previous night. They were all crying crocodile tears saying they loved me and hated what I was doing to myself and them. To which I replied "F**k you, you f**kers. You don't understand what I do for all of you ungrateful sons of bitches! I can stop anytime I want! Leave me ALONE." I made all kinds of excuses: if my wife would do me more often I wouldn't drink; if the kids would appreciate what I gave them I wouldn't drink; if I didn't have that crappy job I wouldn't drink…

They said either I could check myself into treatment voluntarily for thirty days, or they had a court order for ninety days, with the sheriff waiting outside in case I got violent (go figure). Well that was in the spring, and I couldn't be in there during Sturgis! They had me over a barrel, and I let them know that in no uncertain terms.

It was my son's crying that did it, and how he said that he used to love me until about ten years ago when this monster took me away, and that he hated to see that monster come home. He used that term many times, and that finally made me agree to go. I came into treatment kicking and screaming, and nothing and nobody was going to change me!

I made it hell for everyone there and reveled in it. They put the toughest counselor on me, an ex-Marine drill instructor, and I fought him tooth and nail—a Texas hardcore biker against a former hardcore alcoholic Marine. Whoowe, did we tear it up!

No man could change me; it took the power of God to do it.

Many years ago I got into the Black Arts to see naked chicks on altars and such, and picked up on some demons myself (or they picked up on me). As long as I lived in anger, resentment, and hatred I was okay. I was doing their bidding. I knew something was wrong, and years later I went to a holy woman out in California for help. She stopped me twenty feet from her house saying, "Don't come in here; you have a lot of demons on you. Go away!" She could see them from there and was afraid. So every time during treatment when I got a glimmer of something good, they would come at me with a vengeance. That stuff is real and don't mess with it, I tell people. After one particularly shattering bout with them, I was outside smoking a cigarette and shaking like a leaf when one of the other patients suggested I go to church. "Yeah right, every war in the world was started by religion, priests f**king little boys, you can shove that horse crap!" the demons exclaimed through my mouth.

But I went.

I was willing to sacrifice a chicken in the pale moonlight if I had to. I even went to a Native American Inipi Ceremony, a sweat lodge where it gets over two hundred degrees and you can't wear any metal 'cause it will burn your skin. I damn near died in there and saw visions of different shields to help me fight the evil spirits.

While sitting in church I felt safe to think about all the pain I had caused myself and those around me, and I started bawling like a baby. Here was a 260 pound biker, with all my pins and patches of death heads, Nazi SS emblems, my shades, black bandana, the works (my costume to intimidate and strike fear into anyone I came across) with tears streaming down my face.

They had a baptism and the preacher said anyone was welcome. I thought about it for a second and then the demons came up with all kinds of reasons why I couldn't— hadn't worn underwear since '72, etc. (I know, too much information). The preacher said, "We have shorts and shirts in the back for anyone who is interested." Well I went for it, and all the other patients figured I would be the last one to do that. When I came out of that water I knew I didn't have to fight the battle anymore, that a power greater than myself would take over. I felt I was dirty before and now I was clean. Can I hear an AMEN brother?

That was about four years ago, and since then I have found out what true freedom is all about.

I now work at that same inpatient treatment center I went to; I'm using my wounds to help heal others. Tell me there ain't a God! I also do outpatient mentoring for people fresh out of prison for using meth.

I went to college for alcohol and drug studies, so I have all my credentials for counselor status, not to mention fifty-three years of "field research" in alcohol and drug addiction. There isn't much anyone can throw at me that I haven't done. I've still got the long hair, beard, and tattoos, but a lot of patients identify with it. If there is hope for me there is hope for anybody.

When I went into treatment I was literally digging ditches, cursing my fate, saying, "Thank God I'm an alcoholic." I didn't know what I was going to do when I got out, but through the grace of God I run a custom motorcycle shop helping people fulfill their dreams, and I specialize in helping handicapped people get back in the wind. Go to www.freebirdcustommotorcycles.com to see what I'm up to. I also sell chaps, jackets, saddlebags, and parts all over the planet. I write for various worldwide publications, such as www.bikerhotline.com. I now ride with nothing on my back spurring me on to destruction. I notice every tree and plant and am grateful for my pony pulling me along in God's beautiful world. I used to put all that time, effort, and money into building those scooters only to ride them from bar to bar, paranoid of the cops 'cause I was usually drunk and carrying drugs.

The freedom to ride anywhere I want is priceless. You can't enjoy the ride if you are constantly afraid.

When I'm sitting at a stoplight on one of my customs, people say, "Nice bike." I reply, "Thank you, it's a gift… from God!" Everything is a gift from God. I hope I never forget that. I live in service to my higher power and others, and am grateful to be allowed to do that. I get on my knees every morning and night asking God how I can be useful and to help me with my shortcomings, anger, resentments, health, and the health (physical and emotional) of others.

I have been blessed with meeting others who feel the same way I do. I have more fun at Sturgis—no, not fun; I had a lot of superficial fun at the expense of others—now it is joy, which is a lot deeper and longer lasting, since I've been in recovery than I thought possible. I can't say "Thank you, God!" enough to show my appreciation.

It was a fluid gathering at Wayne and Carolyn's place. Some, like me, had just been introduced and were invited to stay, while others had been coming for years.

Riders from all over the US, Canada, and even a couple from Australia who were touring the country in a van, came and went throughout the week. At one point I counted forty tents and a half-dozen campers nestled among the trees around the house. Their eight-car garage was converted into an impromptu clubhouse with room for everyone to relax after a day's ride or to sit in on one of the morning or evening meetings. On a bench against one wall, an endless spread of simple food miraculously appeared; I had the first peanut butter and jelly sandwich I'd eaten in decades along with a handful of pretzels for dinner my first night there. On another wall a bunch of extension cords and electric outlets gave everyone a chance to keep their phones, cameras, and computers charged. A bathroom in one corner was reserved for the ladies—the guys had a port-a-potty under a deck by the house—and a shower next to a washer and dryer in the opposite corner allowed everyone to stay hygienically tolerable. A bunch of recovery-related literature from

THE "CLUBHOUSE" AT WAYNE AND CAROLYN'S PLACE IN STURGIS

various fellowships—daily meditation books, big books, and some religious pamphlets someone had brought in—shared equal space on coffee tables alongside road atlases, travel guides, and maps of the local riding area. I stayed five nights, and everyone I met was someone I'd invite to my own home for dinner.

Finding that refuge of serenity and sanity amongst the chaos of the rally—with the town of Sturgis a few miles to the east, and to the west, hundreds of miles of the most beautiful roads in America leading through the Black Hills to interesting places like Mount Rushmore, Devils Tower, the Needles Highway, the historic town of Deadwood, and countless other worthy destinations—was a true blessing.

I hope heaven is that perfect.

5

STURGIS IS AN ALL-OUT celebration of Biker culture. The bikes are Harleys; the sounds are amplified; the colors are brightly reflected off shiny chrome; the dress codes are leather and lots of tattoos for guys, and less leather, lots of skin, and nicer tattoos for ladies; the bars are busy; the streets and roads are crowded; and the theme is constant motion. It's a mecca for American bikers—everyone who rides owes it to themselves to make a pilgrimage to Sturgis at least once in a lifetime. This was the Seventieth Annual Black Hills Motorcycle Rally; officials later calculated more than six hundred thousand bikes rolled into the area.

I certainly was in the minority on my Beemer; I probably could have counted the number of bikes I saw that weren't Harleys, but I never felt out of place among all the "bikers"—the direct descendants of the post-war motorcycle club scene.

BIKERS ON MAIN STREET IN STURGIS

Motorcycle clubs have always been part of Sturgis and the American motorcycle scene. Sturgis was begun by the Jackpine Gypsies Motorcycle Club as a race with nine competitors and a couple dozen spectators in 1938. The races are still held, but I bet most rally goers aren't even aware of them.

As with anything that has lasted seven decades, motorcycle clubs have evolved, and out of that transformation, "The American Biker" came roaring down the road and into our culture. The image of today's biker was born out of that staged photograph from Hollister, California. The guy in that picture wasn't even a member of the club he was supposed to be representing—The Boozefighters. I had an appointment with Bill Hayes, a current member of that club and the author of *The Original Wild Ones: Tales of the Boozefighters*

Motorcycle Club and the more recent *American Biker: The History, The Clubs, The Lifestyle, The Truth.* The heavy traffic and general confusion in Sturgis kept us from meeting as we'd planned, but we did manage a long phone conversation about the history of motorcycle clubs in the US. Basically there have been three variants of clubs that can be best defined by the time period in which they were formed.

The pre-war motorcycle clubs were primarily social clubs with a focus on riding or racing. The Jackpine Gypsies are one of few remaining clubs from that era. Riders didn't have television or the Internet in those days; they had each other and a common interest. They got together to share their love of bikes with other like-minded friends. They really were no different than members of yacht clubs, gardening clubs, bridge clubs, or even church groups of the day, except their passion was loud, fast, and dangerous. Other than that most of them blended into society and their community like any other citizen.

After World War II, many returning soldiers couldn't just turn off the adrenaline that had been their lifeblood in the heat of battle. Having spent their youth living on the edge of life and death, they needed excitement and found it on motorcycles. Having risked their lives for their country, they'd earned the right to live as they pleased—hard and fast. Their military backgrounds influenced the structure of the clubs they formed. Membership was earned— these guys wanted to be around people they knew they could trust their lives with. Their bikes, military-surplus Harleys and Indians made faster by hopping up and stripping down, became known as bobbers. Their club emblem was their uniform. Through their shared experience they bonded and formed a brotherhood, a fellowship.

And they wanted to have fun. Eventually the press and politicians decided they were having too much fun and the clubs were pulled out of the back alleys into America's living rooms through (mostly) sensationalized news reports and political speeches that began with that single 1947 photo from Hollister. They became famous and infamous at the same time, and the next generation of club members embraced the infamy, which, with time, replaced the shared experience of war the original club members had. The newer, younger members bonded as bikers. They reveled in their vilification and threw it back in society's face. The stripped down bobbers became outrageous choppers; the club emblem became a sacred patch; club membership became the "Lifestyle"; and honor and respect for one's brothers became the highest law of the club— one to live and die by, one that when carried to its extreme trumps the law of society, like the old "Code of the West."

There is a romantic attraction for the outcast, the rebel, and the outlaw, and a primal respect for men who live free by their own rules. Every American biker, to some degree or another, no matter how, what, or where he rides, believes he carries a piece of the rebel and a spark (a spark that sometimes fans into the open flame of a Zippo lighter next to a short fuse on a keg of gunpowder) of freedom out onto to the open road. That's the fellowship that every rider joins just by throwing a leg over the saddle of a bike and heading out the driveway. There are many different levels of commitment to that fellowship varying from the weekend recreational rider to the patch holder in a one-percenter club.

Although most riders don't belong to clubs, the leather-clad biker on a big Harley conjures up the image of smoldering, on-the-edge danger to the public eye. The one-percenter clubs get all the attention in the papers, on the nightly news, and from film and television writers, but there are hundreds of other motorcycle clubs that, despite looking like "outlaw bikers" to the uninitiated, have more in common with the pre-war clubs than their image may imply. There are clubs formed around religious affiliations, occupations, veterans groups, bike brands, charities, race or gender, types of bikes or riding styles, racing or stunting, and hundreds of other associations, such as police officers, honor guards for military funerals, and clean and sober clubs. There is a defined hierarchy with established protocols in place to keep peace among the various clubs. I'm not a joiner, but have taken a few rides with a chapter of a clean and sober club near my home in South Florida called the Alternative MC with a friend, Cajun Joe, who is a member. I've gained a genuine respect for them and their commitment to each other and the lifestyle as they live it.

Riding to the Black Hills is a trip back to a part of the Old West where that romanticized vision of the American spirit of independence and freedom originated. Western legend Wild Bill Hickok hung out (and died) in the town of Deadwood just outside of Sturgis; Calamity Jane is buried next to him at a nearby cemetery. It doesn't take much imagination to picture today's riders as their modern day equivalents riding through those same hills on big, loud Harleys instead of horses.

There is so much to do at Sturgis that I never had to plan ahead. Each of the four days I spent there just evolved naturally into a perfect complement of recovery, fellowship, and adventure. Kevin, the rider from Florida who introduced me to the camp, invited me to join him and his nineteen-year-old daughter Krista, who rode on the back of his Glide, and another friend of his, Jim, for a ride out to the Devils Tower National Monument on my first day there. Kevin found recovery at a clubhouse a mile or so from my house in Miami six years before Krista was born; she's one of those who kids grew up inside the rooms and was touched by the miracle of recovery without having to personally experience the pain and devastation of active addiction. Kevin has been going to Sturgis for years and knows the area well; this was Krista's second trip with him. We headed out right after the morning meeting and rode into Wyoming on I-90, but soon turned off the interstate onto twisty two-lane state roads that run through a few small towns and past many impromptu campgrounds and bars while circling around the Devils Tower National Monument area.

KEVIN

I was born in 1959 and grew up in Glen Cove, New York on Long Island. My dad worked for NY Bell and my mom was a dental hygienist. I have one older sister, Karen. We had a good childhood and were raised in an average middle class neighborhood. I first realized my attraction to motorcycles at an early age, when my Aunt Joan bought me a toy electric motorcycle policeman with flashing lights. I was hooked.

I used the money from my first communion and confirmation to buy a second-hand mini bike from my cousin Tommy. Not being able to ride on the streets legally, I was forced by my parents to ride in a small bocce ball court on the side of our house. After a few years I was allowed to walk my bike a mile to ride in an undeveloped field. Of course there were the times when my parents were out that I would throw caution to the wind and blast around the neighborhood.

My friend Joe got a green KZ 50 that had three gears. Watching him wind that little bike out was a thrill. My uncle Nick gave me an Italian 50 cc bike that was missing a back wheel. I would get it started in our basement and sit on it dreaming of banging through the gears like my buddy Joe. Dad wasn't a wrench and the bike never got the back wheel.

KEVIN AND KRISTA ON THE ROAD TO THE DEVILS TOWER

In high school I followed my sister's lead and became a lifeguard. In the winters I would work various jobs after school. That's when I also started drinking—working hard and partying hard. I wanted to buy a Suzuki 380 with ram air and needed a cosigner for a loan. My mother put her foot down, but thank God my grandmother cosigned for me. That was the best summer of my life.

One day after work as a lifeguard at Crescent Beach, I drank two beers with a couple of friends. Since I was late for my second job parking cars at Glen Head Country Club, I was racing home to change my clothes when a man blew through a stop sign. I hit the side of his car doing sixty miles per hour. Witnesses said I flew as high as the telephone poles and landed fifty feet from the car. The two beers probably helped my landing, but caused the events that led to the accident. In retrospect this was the first time that drinking caused a problem in my life.

In the hospital my mom made me promise no more bikes, and I did. But two nights later with only chipped bones and road rash, I was on the back of my buddy George's 750 Honda. I asked him to give me a ride to get the fear out and it worked. I did keep the promise to my mom for a few years and didn't buy a bike.

I started drinking more and tried many other forms of self-medication. After a failed attempt at college and a few odd jobs, I ended up in Miami working for Southern Bell. I also got a part-time job as a doorman at a strip club. Miami, the eighties—need I say more?

I was at the height of my drinking when I bought a 750 Yamaha Special. The blackout rides were one of the catalysts for my recovery. In a short period of time I was arrested three times due to my drinking and bizarre decision-making.

It was November 21, 1985, and I was standing on the front lawn of a customer's house when the miracle happened. I had a broken hand from punching a wall. My latest girlfriend had just left me. I drove a 1970 Maverick and my motorcycle had a seized engine. I made a called that saved my life and probably others—I ended up at a treatment center in a mental hospital and was released twenty-eight days later. I had already read the big book and had been going to twelve-step meetings. I dove into recovery with a passion.

I was in my fourth month of recovery when I was run over by a boat while scuba diving. I spent two months in the hospital and was operated on twenty-four times in a four-year period. My right foot had to be amputated; my right arm had been torn off, but was successfully reattached.

Every day my sponsor or other people in recovery showed up to give me strength. Twice they brought a meeting to me at the hospital—a real meeting with twenty-five to thirty-five people in my room. For anyone struggling with the God thing—this is what happens when God gets into the picture.

While I was in treatment, my roommate was Joe and my appointed big brother was Randy. We became friends and have remained friends for the past twenty-five years. They were sent to me by God himself. Randy worked at the hospital where I recovered from my accident. He would sneak me out in a wheelchair and roll me to meetings half a mile away from the hospital. He checked on me daily and remains my big brother to this day. Joe owned an orthopedic shop in Miami and made prosthetic limbs. I have never in my life before or since met someone who makes prosthetics. Joe had been my roommate for a month, and has been making my legs ever since.

After several years in recovery from addiction and the accident I married my first wife Debby and moved to Bunnell, Florida. We had two daughters, Krista, now nineteen, and Jamie, now sixteen. We live on twenty acres and that is where I was able to introduce my daughters to motorcycles. Krista now rides a Yamaha 400 and has been to Sturgis with me twice.

Debby and I divorced when the kids were very young. I now live with my present wife Beth, who rides a Softail Deluxe. I presently ride an Excelsior Henderson and an Electric Glide Classic. Beth is another godsend. We plan yearly motorcycle trips and are living the dream.

We got engaged in the Painted Desert while on a motorcycle trip, and got married on the side of a mountain in Red Lodge, Montana; our honeymoon was a riding trip through Yellowstone and Sturgis. I often kid the newcomers that if they stay in recovery for one year, they get a Harley.

My wife is a hardcore rider. One morning we had plans to go on a poker run. I looked out the window and told her it was thirty-five degrees out. When I went back into the room she had tears running down her face. I asked her what was wrong, and she said, "You're not going to want to ride." I hugged her, leathered up, and we rode.

Like recovery, if I get too far from riding something in me dies a little, so I think I'll hit a meeting today, and most likely take a ride too.

KRISTA

My name is Krista. I am a nineteen-year-old girl who has grown up in the back of the rooms and on the back of my dad's bike. Now I ride my own motorcycle, and one day my kids will ride behind me, just like I did for so many years with my father.

My mother used to bring me to twelve-step meetings starting back when she was still breastfeeding me. My mom has been in recovery for twenty-three years and my dad for twenty-four, so both of my parents had solid recovery by the time I was born. I realized what the steps meant when I was eight years old.

I remember being a little kid playing with Barbie dolls and seeing someone detoxing on our couch. In my lifetime there have always been people in and out of our house struggling to find recovery. I grew up hearing the phone ring at two-o-clock in the morning—sometimes earlier, sometimes later—with someone upset and about to relapse.

My mother has helped hundreds, if not thousands, of people on their journey to recovery. I have seen women and men, fat and skinny, short and tall, white and black change their lives. No matter who you are or what you have gone through, recovery is always available. My mother used to say that her job is to help anyone seeking recovery. She said, "I am responsible to be there whenever anyone, anywhere wants the hand of recovery." That is what she was taught in her early days, and I respect that. I've seen her live those words. Listening to the stories of people's lives and hearing what they have been though has motivated me to stay away from kids my own age who seem to drink or get high too much.

We live near Daytona, and I grew up watching bikers come to town for Bike Week every year. My dad and his friends would go on these clean and sober motorcycle runs. At Bike Week we see other bikers drunk, running around on Main Street. We see them pulled over by cops. We read about them in papers when they crash and get hurt when riding and drinking. It is sad but it is very true.

Every year during Bike Week in Daytona, my dad holds a hog roast out on the property we own. It is a place to hang out, eat, dance, and enjoy a live band without worrying about a drunk hitting your bike or throwing up on your shoes. It is a place to meet people who are not wasted.

It's a place to make memories. It's somewhere you can bring your kids and show them Bike Week and not be disgusted.

We have biker games. We have more biker games than most places do because there is no drinking, so we don't have to worry about people doing stupid things. I love the life of a biker. It is a blast—the wind in my hair, the smells I don't get to smell when riding in a car, the sound of the gravel under my tires, the feel of the sun beating down on my back.

When I'm on my bike nothing matters—not my home life, not my problems. I become one with my bike. That's how it is for my dad also. I think that helps him stay in recovery. When he is having a rough day he gets the guys together and goes for a ride.

My life has always been about bikes: building them, fixing them, washing them, and riding them. I started riding as soon as I learned how to ride my bicycle without training wheels. I started on a little 50cc bike, then I got a 75, then a 125—all dirt bikes because I was too young to ride on streets then. A week after I turned sixteen and got my driver's license, I took the test to get my motorcycle license. That way I could go to Sturgis with my dad.

I was sixteen when I got my first motorcycle. My dad and I rebuilt an old Yamaha 400 sports bike and gave it a custom paint job. Then we drove our truck with the motorcycles in the back to the other side of the US—a two-thousand mile drive—just to ride in South Dakota. We stayed at a campground for those in recovery that we now stay at every year. They hold twelve-step meetings at that campground every day, one in the morning and one at night. There are people of all ages. Everyone pitches in and we buy food and donate money to a charity in town.

I think it is beautiful to see a new person come in and pick up that white chip and look around and say, "I'm ready, guys." Lots of people never make it. I've learned we can only give them as much strength as they are willing to take and absorb. You can't force anyone into recovery; that is one of people's biggest mistakes. That person has to really want it deep down in the bottom of his or her heart and soul. It has a lot to do with having faith, not only in God, but in yourself and the people around you—there is always someone to hold you up when your knees go weak with temptation. There is no such thing as one drink or one shot. There is no "I'll stop tomorrow." There is only today. I've learned recovery is about honesty, faith, love, and tolerance. I hope everyone rides fast and takes chances in life—just be smart about it. Recovery works; I've known that all my life. Pass it on…

Our first stop for gas was an eye-opener. Every pump had at least five or six bikes lined up waiting for a turn to fill up. It must have taken half-an-hour for the three us to get fuel. Back on the road all I could see ahead of or behind us were thousands of motorcycles riding in a staggered pattern. Occasionally some fool would rush past the line of bikes and crowd in when oncoming traffic forced him back into the formation. One stupid idiot on a big bagger came barging through the middle of the pack, swerving in and out and between all of us who were riding in an orderly manner. For the most part everyone rode well, but there were those few exceptions that scared me. I'm not a big fan of group riding and tried to avoid it for the rest of my time at the rally.

BIKERS ON THE ROAD DURING THE BLACK HILLS RALLY

The traffic that day was exceptionally heavy because one of the towns on the way, Hulett, was sponsoring its annual "Panty-Free Wednesday" celebration. From what I was told, it's gotten tamer in the past couple years—women are required to at least wear thongs and body paint to cover their breasts while out on the streets now—but it still draws quite a crowd.

Many people recognize the Devils Tower from the 1977 science fiction film *Close Encounters of the Third Kind.* But other than a few bewildered tourists who were getting a surprise introduction to the Black Hills Rally, there weren't any aliens—just bikers. It was brutally hot and I gratefully accepted a bottle of ice-cold water and a couple pamphlets from some members of a Christian motorcycle club, The Hellfighters Christian Ministries, who were set up at a number of places around the area during the rally offering relief from the sun's heat in this life, and salvation from the heat of hell in the next. Their beliefs are different than mine, but I do respect their service. God bless them.

Kevin and Krista had to hurry back for an appointment in Rapid City, so Jim and I split from them and stopped for dinner and hit a Walmart on the way back. He got some photos downloaded from his camera, and I picked up some glue to repair one of my boots. The sole had come unglued and was flopping in the wind; I repaired it with the glue and some clamps borrowed from Wayne's workbench back at camp.

I rolled into camp just as it was getting dark and the evening meeting was starting.

I've been in recovery for close to three decades now, and it would be impossible to calculate how many meetings I've been to. My recovery is the single most important thing in my life—more important than my marriage, my family, any job, my motorcycle, even my dog—because without recovery all those other things would be at risk. If I started using again it probably wouldn't take long for me to lose interest in anything other than the next drink or drug. I probably average, between the two fellowships I go to, three to five meetings a week. I don't think any of my friends outside of the fellowships know I'm involved in recovery. They know I don't drink or do drugs—when we go out for dinner they may have a beer or glass of wine and I'll drink water or, very occasionally, a non-alcoholic beer. It's not important for them to know all the details; they just know me for who I am today. My recovery is quiet and personal, and as long as I keep doing the right things in my life it works perfectly for me.

At home I'd never go to two meetings a day, but while at Wayne and Carolyn's place I woke up to a meeting every morning

ME ON THE ROAD TO THE DEVILS TOWER

and managed to, without planning it, make it back in time for all the evening meetings. It just worked out that way. Those were special meetings. No matter how anyone justifies it, riding a motorcycle cross country to the rally in Sturgis is an indulgence; I'm very aware how fortunate I am to have a wife who understands my need to do such a thing and that I have the time and means to do so. It's one of the gifts of life I've earned by living in recovery. And I believe everyone there felt equally privileged and blessed to live with that same sentiment of freedom after having been ensnared in the desperate slavery of addiction.

All meetings have different "personalities," sometimes based on the people attending the meeting, sometimes influenced by the location, format, defined objective, or history of the meeting. Occasionally a strong personality will set the tone, or someone's particular problem, victory, relapse, anniversary, joke, or whatever will do so. All meetings are different, just like bars. I didn't like every bar I walked into, but I could get what I needed, and I'd stay as long as it served my purpose. All twelve-step meetings offer the hope of recovery, but sometimes the message is stronger than others, and these meetings in the impromptu clubhouse in Carolyn and Wayne's garage served up high-octane gratitude that caused more than one hardened biker to choke up while sharing about how good life is.

There seemed to be a core group at the camp and a number of others who weren't staying there, but dropped in for the meetings.

One night a guy named Chuck rode in on a Road King with a guitar strapped on the back. He's a specialist in whatever it is he does for work and travels to jobs all over North America on his bike for different contract jobs. And he's a modern day troubadour of the Woody Guthrie style, writing songs he catches out of the wind while traveling on his bike. He entertained us singing around a campfire with songs of life, lost loves, and the road. The next day he and I went for a ride together through an area called Spearfish Canyon, another National Scenic Byway slightly north and west of Sturgis, and returned by way of Deadwood.

CHUCK

I guess I should start off by saying that motorcycles have not always been part of my recovery process, and at times have been more closely related to my disease of addiction. But nonetheless, they have also played an important part in my recovery. I will attempt to relate that part of my riding experience.

In the early part of 1983, I was at the bottom and had no home, no wheels, and was being ordered by the US Navy to attend their most stringent addiction treatment facility in Jacksonville, Florida. My wife had left me, taking our four-year-old son, and I had just barely squeaked out of going to prison at Leavenworth for at least six months.

So under duress I went to rehab, and something magical happened there that has changed my life up to the time of this writing—I got into recovery.

Right out of treatment I went to the Honda shop and purchased a 1983 Magna V45. Then I started attending meetings and would ride my bike (my only transportation at the time), and frequently I would give one of my buddies in the program a ride. (That was before we became homophobic and it wasn't cool to let a guy ride with you.) I rode that bike to hundreds of meetings, sometimes two or three a day. I met several others who had bikes, and we would hang out after meetings and ride over to HoJo's for coffee. I had a blast on that bike and was able to make the meetings that I needed—then came adversity. Just after Thanksgiving of '83, a car pulled out in front of me and totaled the Magna. I also got messed up in the deal and have physical problems relating to that wreck to this day.

Now let me back up a bit, because I must give credit where credit is due. When I bought the Magna, I had no credit and yet I was able to purchase that bike with credit. Then after I broke my leg in the crash and was on my way to recovering, some of my Navy buddies I rode with would deploy (as good sailors do) and leave me their bikes to take care of while they were gone, so I always seemed to have a bike at my disposal. This seems like a God thing to me!

CHUCK SINGING ABOUT LIFE ON THE ROAD

So during the interim, I had a friend sell me a BSA that he had disassembled and put in a box, and we rebuilt that rascal—don't ask me what model it was, because as near as we could figure, there were parts from three different models involved. I can't describe what building this bike did for me, but I gained knowledge and confidence, and was learning how to enjoy just being human, without the use of substances.

Well, not too long after I got the Beeser on the road, I had a near-miss accident and that shook me up pretty bad. I was still recovering from my crash on the Magna and decided to stop riding for a while.

That lasted for about three years and then the opportunity to buy a 1978 Super Glide Harley, an old Shovelhead, came along and I had just found out that I could probably get a loan from a source I didn't think even existed at that time. So I bought that Shovel, and as a result I made some more friends in recovery that I might have never met.

I had the Shovel for about three years, then my wife at the time and I started a business and we were strapped for cash, so I let the bike go. Funny thing about that— the business and the marriage also—I should have kept the bike. That experience probably influenced some later judgment calls along the same lines.

Then began the dark times: my marriage ended; I was out of work; my truck died; and I ended up homeless. Fortunately some kind souls took me in and eventually helped me to get back on my feet. During those days there were no motorcycles for me, and there was a lot of depression.

Apparently God carried me through those times, and there were some good things that happened, as well as some bad decisions on my part. Through it all though, I did not find it necessary to use, and I have found that as long as I manage that then there is always hope.

I married again (number three) and eventually became financially solvent, so when a friend offered me a "deal" on a purple 1978 Super Glide, I thought, sure…why not? Well this one was not such a wonderful deal and I had tons of problems with it (don't know how I stayed in recovery through that one). While on the only road trip I took on that bike, it kept breaking down and my friends wanted to leave me along the road. We stopped at a Harley shop in PA to try to get some new brakes for the bike, and I ended up rolling out of there on a brand-new Road King. This was my first bagger and probably changed my riding for life. I had logged a lot of miles on the various bikes that I owned over the years, but this motorcycle was dependable and comfortable on the long haul and sure ate up the miles.

Now when I am riding I let go of all my stress and stop worrying about life and just enjoy the ride. I don't know of anything else that has this effect on me, and that is probably the biggest reason for my love of riding motorcycles.

About a year and a half after buying the Road King, my marriage was deteriorating quickly, and in the heat of the moment with the battle of the sexes raging around me, I traded that bike for what has become my favorite bike of all time—and in so doing effectively ended my marriage. I am sure some would consider this cold, but I had no peace in that relationship and I was once again faced with the decision to give up something that gives me peace and joy to try to salvage a sinking ship. I could not do it again.

In two-and-a-half years I have logged seventy-three thousand miles on this bike, been to Alaska, all over northwest Canada, and met several people who have had a profound impact on my life (one of whom is the author of this book). I have seen places that I've wanted to see since childhood. I ride alone most of the time, but have friends that I will do the big rides with when possible.

I am a songwriter, and I carry a guitar on my bike and do most of my writing while I am riding.

Every now and then I think to myself…maybe I should give this up and live like normal people; but after just a week or two of not riding, I start looking down the highway and know that my freedom lies out there on the ride.

Another night Scotty and Michelle, a couple of true nomads, rode in for a meeting. Scotty has been living on his bike for seventeen years now, and Michelle for four. Neither has any use for a permanent address other than a place to have their bike registration, driver's license, and cell phone bills mailed to. Both of them live full-time on the road, working whenever something pops up, sometimes following the motorcycle rally circuit and sometimes not, sometimes riding together and sometimes not. Just following whim and weather to whatever adventure waits down the next road.

I also spent some time talking with Tony and Rebecca, a couple from Australia who were exploring the US on an extended vacation. Although they were traveling in a used van they picked up after flying into California, they are true bikers from down under. They met someone along the way who introduced them to Wayne and Carolyn. They both constantly wore open expressions of joy and wonder, like little kids on Christmas morning, knowing they were about to discover some wonderful surprise that day. It was a true pleasure meeting and getting to know them.

TONY

The weather was starting to cool down in our hometown in New South Wales, Australia, so it was time to make tracks to a warmer climate. Thailand was on the agenda until my wife said, "Why don't we go to the United States for the AA International Convention, and we could make it to Sturgis as well?" Being an avid motorcycle enthusiast for more than thirty-five years, I thought "Why not?" This was only six weeks before we were to fly out of Sydney, but as we both have addiction, we still tend to cut things a little short. I call it riding by the seat of my pants, and at times its good because we have learned to be spontaneous (not reckless) in recovery—the difference is now we are "going to" not "running from," even if we leave things late on the planning front. Still, we managed to find accommodation in San Antonio at the eleventh hour. Our recovery is like that; we always land on our feet when we're on the right path.

Typical addicts, we don't do life by half measures, so we thought, "We've got the ticket; let's go for a few months." We landed at LAX in June 2010 and stayed with a member of our twelve-step fellowship. He rode an old Softail and showed us a great time. My wife and I both have home groups and we get as many as twenty people at our meeting on a good day, but the night we hit Pacific Group we thought we were at the annual convention. There were over five hundred people there, and the "wow factor" hit me; there is so much recovery in LA.

We flew into Las Vegas to buy a car for the rest of our trip and ended up at the disabled veterans car lot, where we picked a 1996 Chrysler Town and Country van for our

US tour. After some new tires and a full service, we headed south to San Antonio, staying with like-minded people along the way. I stopped at every Harley-Davidson store to buy a T-Shirt, and we saw so many bikers heading to the convention, often stopping to chat about our common interests in bikes and recovery. It was cool to see so many bikers in recovery, as we really don't have anything like that in Australia.

We arrived in San Antonio and found our billets at one of the Catholic colleges. After working out the schedule, we met some fantastic people to go to the meetings with and found plenty of things to keep us occupied. We used our Roadside America Guide and the Internet for points of interest along the way. The opening ceremony was a sight to behold—over six hundred thousand people in recovery saying the Serenity Prayer was so powerful that it made the hair stand up on the back of my neck. We didn't get to many meetings because they were packed out, but we found smaller places to go with our recovery friends and visited the Sober Ranch and Sober City. The last event was the old timers meeting, for members who have forty-plus years in recovery. They shared their experience, strength, and hope with the rest of us, and again, "wow" wouldn't be enough to explain how it made us feel to see these fantastic examples of what it can be like to be in long-term recovery.

After the convention we headed north for Sturgis, South Dakota for the Seventieth Annual Motorcycle Rally. There were over six hundred thousand bikers transiting through the Black Hills to get to that event. We found Wayne and Carolyn's place to stay at, and for us that was the icing on the cake. What fantastic examples these two members are, and well over fifty fellow bikers from different twelve-step fellowships stayed there from all over North America and Canada (and now Australia!). This year was their forty-second wedding anniversary, and a few members arranged a banner and a small surprise. At the ranch we had two twelve-step meetings every day, and that was just what these Aussies needed. We enjoyed the ranch and the company so much that we stayed for a few days after all of the other bikers left, just to get to know our hosts a little better. While we were there we bonded with so many bikers, but one couple became so close that we were "adopted" by them, Ron and Carol from Sioux Falls. This wonderful couple loaned us a Harley to ride with them, so off we went all through the Black Hills and Badlands. It was just what I needed, some Harley therapy. I loved every minute of it. We never had to wear a helmet, so we felt like part of the open road. What freedom! In Australia we have to wear helmets (it's a mandatory law in every state), but that will be the hardest thing to go back to. We went up to Canada then came back to visit Ron and Carol and stayed with them in Sioux Falls. Their housemate, Jim, a fellow biker in recovery, loaned us his newer Softail for the ten days of our stay so we could tour around the adjoining states. We had a blast, and their hospitality was second to none—a great bunch of friends who are coming down under next year so we can show them our slice of heaven.

To be in the US and to be riding a bike was just a dream of mine when I drank. In 1986 I lost my driver's license for the fifth time, and with that I lost my Harley (because my license was suspended for another two years). At that time I was married, had a young family, and was in the military. I couldn't afford to buy a bike again, and my wife had had enough. The bike going was the price

I paid for f***ing up again. I was always going to stop if things got too bad, but denial ran deep in the mind of this addict. So the drinking story went on for another eighteen years and things did get bad—a whole lot worse than even I could have imagined. I woke up in a military hospital on life support. My marriage was long over, my now-adult kids couldn't stand the sight of me, and my career of close to thirty years was all but finished.

After getting out of the hospital I ended up in a rehab where I was to find the fellowship that was to save my life and give me hope. Right from the start I did what I was told and slowly things in my life picked up. I did the ninety-in-ninety thing, and bang, I found what I was looking for—a chance to begin to live a life I had long since forgotten that I dreamt of. My marriage had failed, but in time, I gained back the respect of my kids because my fellowship taught me to do what I said I was going to do when I said I was going to do it. I am the dad they always wanted because I am truly present in their lives today.

Now I have grandkids who love me and want me in their little lives. I go to three to four meetings every week, and I have done the steps to the best of my ability. I have been blessed to have found a new wife who is in the fellowship, and we share a full life together and travel as much as we can. We do this because we are in recovery and wherever we go, we have found fellowship. That's a must for this pair of addicts, because without our "spiritual medication" we are doomed to fail. We both know that if we are put into the wrong set of circumstances, we will drink against our will, so we holiday where there are meetings, and that's a safe bet for us.

Being able to pursue our passions is a byproduct of being in recovery, and staying in recovery equals going to meetings, whether we like it or not. We both know that to be true because we have seen too many people who stop going to meetings, and it's not too long before they're either loaded or dead.

The meetings in the US are a little different from the ones in Australia and getting used to them has been an adjustment, but we have learned to fit in wherever we go, because our fellowship works just fine wherever it is. It's our job to change to fit the circumstances, not to change the circumstances to fit us. At home our meetings run for ninety minutes, and we tend to follow an "ID format" (what it was like, what happened, and what it is like now). People usually speak for ten minutes and are called to the front by the secretary/chairperson. Usually only the preamble and "how it works" is read, and we always close with the Serenity Prayer. But I can see why the US meetings run the way they do, because of the volume of members in attendance. The biggest difference has been the smoking in meetings, as all meetings in Australia are now smoke-free.

By doing what I have done I have been able to buy three Harleys over the last five years. I fix them up, and then I sell them to start all over again. I ride every day and attend as many bike rallies as I can. I ride mostly with drinkers, but it is never a problem because I know where that next drink will take me. The first thing to go would be my wife, then the bikes and kids. Stuff the "yets," it's the "agains" I don't want back in my life.

We enjoyed our stay in the US and Canada because it gave us a chance to knock off three of the things on my bucket list—a convention, Sturgis, and a belated honeymoon with my beautiful wife. Meeting some of the coolest people in recovery was just a bonus. I'm hoping to get back to Sturgis again, and maybe bring some more Aussies with us next time. The biker culture needs to know that we're here, in recovery, from every country and every walk of life.

One day I rode alone to look at the bars on the east side of Sturgis, but that area was too crowded and noisy for me so I just kept going east on South Dakota Highway 34, which runs parallel to I-90. I wanted to go to the Badlands National Park; some distant relatives on my mother's side used to farm somewhere in the Badlands and I wanted to see it. I figured I'd stay on 34 and catch a road running south to 90 and make my way to the park that way. The road caught me by surprise and I ended up traveling more than a hundred miles before finding a right turn off 34. The ride was fun, though. Running through the open prairie, the road is mostly straight with just the right amount of gentle hills and mild curves to keep it interesting. I trusted fate, twisted my throttle, and held the bike at a speed that would have gotten very expensive if some local sheriff had decided to discuss it with me. Even with a stop to check my map in the unincorporated roadside community of Howes, where a single building serves as the post office, general store, gas station, community center, and rest area, the run took less than an hour. I asked where the restrooms were at Howes and was directed to a pair of outhouses in the middle of a large gravel parking area. The walls were thick poured concrete and the doors were heavy steel with deep dents from bullets that hadn't penetrated through to the inside. I've never seen an outhouse built that solid—the old proverbial brick facilities could never stand up against these.

ROADSIDE SCENE IN WYOMING

After riding through the Badlands I stopped for gas at a small independent station that allowed me to pour, according to the numbers on the pump, almost seven gallons into my not-empty six-and-a-half gallon tank. Some battles are not worth fighting, and I rode away without pointing out the "discrepancy" to the management.

The next day I took another solo ride. This time I headed south from Sturgis on the emptiest roads I could find and ended up at Mount Rushmore National Park, then tried to continue on to the Needles Highway, a famous road that runs through Custer State Park where a herd of fifteen hundred buffalo roam free and wild burros wander through the lines of cars begging for food. But I got impatient with the traffic, bailed out, and spent the day exploring less popular destinations. Sometime I will go back to the Black Hills a few weeks before or after the rally so I can ride the wonderful roads and see the sights without fighting my own impatience and the traffic of half a million of my brothers.

Later that evening, which was to be my last night at camp, I decided to head out toward Seattle instead of going straight back to Miami. I was looking at my map and asking others about some of the roads through Montana when Mark, a rider from southern Indiana and a member of the Christian Motorcyclist Association, asked if he could join me for as far as Yellowstone. We talked for a bit and agreed to hit the road right after the morning meeting.

I called my wife and told her I'd be a week later than first planned, did a load of laundry, said goodbye to some of my new friends, and crawled into my tent and went to sleep.

6

I HAVEN'T FOUND ANYONE with the same size fuel tank or the same size bladder as me. I don't like to ride with other people on long trips.

I don't like having a passenger with me on long rides either. When my wife and I want to do a ride together someplace nice, I will ride there by myself and she'll fly in with all her gear. I'll meet her at the airport and we'll spend a week or two doing short day rides and camp around an area, then she will fly back home and I'll continue my ride. We've done this in New England, the Southwest, the Pacific Northwest, and around the Great Lakes. It's great for both of us; I get to spend time alone in the saddle on the way to and from our rendezvous, and she doesn't have to get bored riding on the back of the bike for ten or twelve hours at a time.

I wasn't sure if I wanted to ride with Mark as we headed west out of Sturgis on I-90. Before leaving we'd discussed our route, our riding habits, and how close to the speed limit we wanted to keep it. I usually try to ride just a bit faster than the prevailing traffic, but not fast enough to draw undue attention to myself. I let Mark lead and found his style was almost perfectly synced with mine. So far, so good. We seemed to be compatible in the way we placed ourselves in our lanes and how we passed other vehicles as well. I was comfortable riding with him. If I hadn't been, I would have made an excuse and bailed.

My original plan for the day was to stay on the interstate for a couple hundred miles to the city of Sheridan, Wyoming, where

SCENE FROM THE BEARTOOTH PASS—
"THE MOST BEAUTIFUL DRIVE (RIDE) IN AMERICA"

I'd jump off onto back roads and wander my way to Red Lodge, Montana and then cross over Beartooth Pass before finding a spot to camp in Yellowstone Park. The Beartooth Pass is another of the scenic byways that's been on my must-ride list for many years. It rises to nearly eleven thousand feet, well above the tree line, and passes through an alpine plateau filled with numerous glacial lakes. Charles Kuralt called it "the most beautiful drive in North America."

Mark preferred the interstate instead of taking a lot of back roads so we agreed to stay on I-90 all the way to Billings, Montana and head to the Beartooth from there. That part of the freeway is a nice ride—just enough curves and hills to keep it from getting boring, like the long trek across South Dakota had been. The weather was cool, so I wore the liners under my riding suit even though the sky was bright and blue without a threat of rain. It was a beautiful morning, and I didn't mind staying on the slab with him for the easy four hundred miles between Sturgis and the entrance to Yellowstone—a relaxing day's ride at my regular pace.

At our first gas stop, though, I realized my schedule might be a bit optimistic. My normal gas stop takes about ten minutes. I fill the tank using a credit card, go inside to use the restroom and clean my face shield, grab a handful of nuts out of my tank bag, guzzle some water, and get back to the road. I went through my routine and was sitting on the bike when Mark came out of the store after prepaying for his gas. Then he went back in for his change after filling and came out with some food and asked me why I was in such a hurry. Going with the flow, I removed my helmet and went inside to get a cup of coffee and came back out to enjoy the morning with him.

Forty-five minutes later we got back on the road. One hundred miles later we stopped in Sheridan to remove a layer of clothes because it had gotten real hot as we dropped down in elevation. One of my personal rules of the road is to never pass up a convenient chance to top off the tank. I've spent too many miles worrying if I would make it to the next station, so we got gas in Sheridan also, then Mark wanted to eat. Somehow, at lunch, we met a guy and his wife who had just come over the Beartooth that morning. They reported it was in the low thirties and cloudy with occasional snow flurries. My instinct was to hurry and make it over the pass before evening hit and it started to get real cold. Mark decided he needed a second cup of coffee.

One of the great blessings of traveling by motorcycle the way I do is that watches and calendars lose all importance. I'd quit paying attention to what day of the week it was. But at lunch I realized it was Sunday and I wanted to call in to my meeting back in Miami later in the day. Making that call was more important than making my arbitrary schedule—I got a second cup of coffee myself. The Beartooth could wait till the next day.

We dawdled over lunch then hit the road again. Just a few miles down the road Mark noticed a historical marker so we stopped to see what and when whatever happened there happened. What happened is probably only important to the small souvenir shop next door that offers tourists a chance to enjoy a few moments of air conditioning after reading the inscription about a soldier's bones that were found somewhere in the area and buried there.

As we were climbing back on our bikes, a van with Canadian plates pulled in and a couple guys got out and came over to talk with us. They were wearing colors from the same club I'd seen hanging out at the gas stations near Sturgis. Mark was worried that they'd give him a hard time because of the Christian Motorcycle Association patch sewn on the back of his jacket, but they just wanted to let their dog go for a walk and break the boredom of their drive back to Vancouver, British Columbia with a little conversation. They ignored

Mark's Harley and asked a lot of questions about my BMW. They knew all about Harleys; the Beemer was new to them.

Back on the highway we only made it a few more miles before seeing the sign to Custer's Battlefield. We stopped and Mark took a tour, sat in on a lecture, and checked out the museum while I listened to my regular Sunday night twelve-step meeting from twenty-five hundred miles and two time zones away over my mobile phone while sitting on the now tranquil battlefield.

We found a campground in the small town of Hardin a little ways past Custer's memorial and waited while another group of riders—two guys and two girls—from the same club we'd met earlier in the day finished checking in. These guys rented a cabin and stayed to themselves; we didn't talk or even acknowledge each other. A cute, young, blond-haired waitress with a piercing in her left eyebrow brought us dinner at a restaurant down the road from the campground. She's studying psychology at Montana State University and is one of the most delightful people I've ever met. Don't remember her name and I know I'll never see her again, but I'll never forget her sparkle and that brief encounter.

The next morning I was up at first light and ready to go as soon as the sun dried the dew off my tent and I had it packed. I wanted to make up for lost miles from yesterday's slow day, and allowed myself to get aggravated while waiting a couple hours for Mark to roll out of his tent and pack up. We managed to get on the road by nine. We had about a hundred miles to Red Lodge—fifty miles of that on I-90 to Billings, where we exited onto US Route 212, a two-lane back road that would carry us to Red Lodge, over the Beartooth, and into Yellowstone. Mark led again, and I wished he'd pick up the pace, but I didn't want to pass him and possibly make him ride faster than he was comfortable doing on his big Harley. I was surprised to see a number of billboard-sized signs planted in the middle of farm fields there in the pristine countryside of rural Montana warning of the dangers of crystal meth. Today I look at places like this part of Montana and think it's such a perfect place that I wouldn't want to dilute the beauty of living there with drugs. But thirty years ago, I probably would have tried to enhance the experience with a joint and a drink. I was glad to be riding through that day.

Half the customers at a local restaurant in Red Lodge appeared to be riders preparing to cross the Beartooth. On a bench outside the restaurant after breakfast, Mark and I pulled on additional layers of clothes. My phone was out of range so I wasn't able to check conditions, but another rider we asked guessed temperatures would be somewhere in the high thirties.

Layered up and gassed up, we headed out and up.

The road is easy. There are plenty of switchbacks, but they are gentle with long, straight sections between them. The weather had changed for the better. The previous day's cold and snow made

LAST GAS BEFORE THE BEARTOOTH

way for clear blue skies and warm temps; we had to de-layer about halfway up to the summit. Mark's pace on the road was perfect, but he wanted to stop at every outlook and wayside to admire the beauty, take photos, and get into lengthy conversations with other people. I wanted to keep moving. At one stop a family from Virginia noticed the Christian Motorcyclist Association patch on his jacket and they discussed scripture for a good half-hour.

I decided to stay with him until we got to the park entrance on the other side then take off on my own. Neither of us has the "right" way to tour. I like to put on lots of miles and Mark likes to explore and visit with people. After I got back home, I called him and we talked about our trips. He'd spent two weeks camping in Yellowstone taking photos, watching wildlife, and getting to know the area. I had breezed through the park on the shortest route in a couple hours, hurrying to the next great must-ride road up in Glacier National Park. I think I'd like to try Mark's method someday, but I don't know when that will be.

My route through the northern part of Yellowstone took me past large herds of bison grazing in meadows off the side of the road. At one area a line of cars were stopped because a number of the huge creatures were standing in the road blocking traffic. One of the beasts decided to wander down the shoulder right past me on my bike. It was close enough that I could have reached over and touched its brown fur, or a horn. I've read about cars, and even RVs, being destroyed by attacking bison, and this guy had my full attention. Park officials advise visitors to stay at least seventy-five feet away from the bison, and I wasn't even that many inches away. Compared to many other motorcycles my bike is large, but it's nothing compared to a full-grown bison. I was ready at the slightest twitch in my direction from him to drop my bike between us and run to any of the cars stopped with me on that road that I usually felt

BISON ON THE SIDE OF THE ROAD IN YELLOWSTONE

superior to and beg for safety inside their secure cage. This wasn't to be my only close encounter with potentially dangerous wildlife on this trip, but at least I got to take some photos of this one.

Leaving the park in the late afternoon through the north entrance at Gardiner, Montana, I headed north on US Route 89 with the intention of stopping early and getting a start toward Glacier in the morning at first light. I noticed a few places to camp, but none of them felt right. The road wound through a valley with the Yellowstone River on my right; the sun, low in the western sky, was blocked by the tall hills on my left, and it was dark enough in the shadows that I had to remove my sunglasses. I slowed to look at a campground down a long, steep hill on a peninsula in the river. I wanted to turn back and spend the night there. It was a place where I could have pitched my tent within a few feet of the river, parked my bike next to the tent, built a fire, and climbed partway back up the hill and taken a photo that would have answered anyone's question when they ask, "Why do you go on these long motorcycle trips?" I could have shown them that picture and said, "That's why I ride." They would have understood.

But something kept pulling me along. I ended up on I-90 again heading straight into the setting sun. Even with my sunglasses back on behind the dark tinted face shield on my helmet, I had to keep my left hand raised up to shade my eyes. I was getting pelted by suicidal bugs, and I was uncomfortably hot. I figured I'd stop in Bozeman and try to reach an old friend who'd moved there after passing through on a motorcycle trip back in the early nineties, but I just rolled past Bozeman also. Finally, after the sun had dropped below the horizon, in the last of the evening's twilight, I found a campground in Three Rivers, Montana that "felt right."

I pulled up to the office and noticed a group of the same motorcycle club I'd been running into since I first got near Sturgis.

I registered in the office, but had to go back out to my bike to fetch my wallet. A couple of the guys from the club came up to me and asked me about my bike—I was getting used to this. We talked for a while then all walked into the office together. The lady said, "Oh, you boys know each other? If you want to camp with them it'll only cost you three dollars instead of twenty-four."

Twenty-one bucks is a tank of gas and a bottle of water; I didn't have a problem sharing a space with them, and one of the guys indicated it was okay, so I camped with the club. It was fully dark by the time I'd gotten my tent set up. They had already crawled into their tents for the night. I bought some snacks in the campground store and cooked a meal of freeze-dried spaghetti on my single-burner camp stove for dinner and went to sleep soon after eating.

In the morning, Sheldon, the president of that chapter and I got into a conversation about my bike and general road talk; I asked about their ride.

"Where you guys heading?" I asked.

"We're going back to Seattle from Sturgis."

"Yea, I'm heading to Seattle too," I said, "I was at Sturgis and now I'm on my way home to Miami, but decided to visit some old friends out there since I'm so close. What part of Seattle are you from?"

"South Seattle," he said.

"I'm originally from there...." The conversation continued and narrowed down; eventually we discovered we'd gone to high school together. We knew each other and used to go to the same parties.

We filled each other in on some old acquaintances we'd stayed in touch with and recalled some old high school stories. I'd graduated in 1974, Sheldon in '76. Our school was wide open back then as far as drugs go. We used to have keg parties in the student parking lot during school hours, and we'd walk through the halls smoking joints. I was constantly getting caught smoking pot, being drunk, or high on acid at school, but never got in trouble for it. I really thought I was getting away with something. On what? On who? Today I have no idea.

Sheldon introduced me to the rest of his chapter and we exchanged phone numbers. They were staying on the interstate all the way west, and I was headed north on back roads toward Glacier; we said goodbye as I walked back to my loaded bike.

Then, out of the blue, Sheldon said, "I've been clean and sober for twenty-five years."

I walked back and we talked a bit more about recovery before I rode out of the campground wondering what the statistical odds are of running into the president of a one-percenter motorcycle club, who was an old high school acquaintance, at a small campground in the middle of Montana, and discovering he and I were both members of the same twelve-step program.

That's why I ride.

SHELDON

I was fourteen years old in the summertime of 1971 when my family and I went from our home in Renton, Washington back to Burley, Idaho for a family reunion.

On our way home we stopped off at the Snake River, right at the site where Evel Knievel was scheduled to jump in two days. I remember looking down over the cliff into the water below, and much to my surprise and the delight of my young eyes, there were some women skinny dipping and splashing around in the water and laughing. Alongside the river were bikers—there must have been over two hundred of them just hanging out, blasting loud music, drinking, smoking, and having fun as they rode around on choppers, squealing the tires against the brown dirt. A couple hundred yards from them the corn and potato fields began, and it was there that I noticed the farmers standing there motionless. They stood clutching rifles and shotguns, staring the bikers and their exhibitionist women down. That is when I knew I had found my calling, my ultimate goal in life. I wanted to become a biker.

Flash forward five years…I am a private in the United States Army stationed in Berlin, Germany. On the first day of my tour I was introduced to heroin—skag as it was more commonly called. I held no reservations or inhibitions as I snorted that first line of white powder; I remember chasing it down with a strong rum and coke. Instantly I was hooked. I was learning urban guerrilla warfare during the day from the military, and at night I was turned loose out onto the wild streets of Berlin. The bars never closed, the alcohol and other drugs began to flow, and within months I had a gram-and-a-half a day habit that was increasing rapidly.

SHELDON, MY FRIEND FROM HIGH SCHOOL

A year into my tour I met two guys called Dirty Bert and Wolf; they belonged to a local motorcycle club called the Barbarian Lords. I began prospecting almost immediately. My childhood dream was coming true. I was a biker in an outlaw biker club and a heroin dealer. Everything was perfect…or so I thought.

The seductive lifestyle of fast bikes, naked women, and the endless supply of booze and heroin came with a price. Two years after joining the club I was court martialed for attempted murder and armed robbery. Things were quickly getting out of hand; ten months later I was busted for dealing heroin. It was in June of 1978 when my commanding officer gave me a choice: I could either be locked up in the stockade or I could go to treatment. The decision was a no-brainer; I told my commanding officer with a grin on my face, "Treatment here I come."

While I was in treatment, the American news show *20/20* was doing a special on the American military. My treatment facility was among the selected few that the reporter Geraldo Rivera and his camera crew visited to interview soldiers. Miles away back home in quiet, peaceful Renton, Washington, the Sunday night routine at my parent's house went on as normal. They sat down to dinner while watching *20/20,* and much to their surprise, their oldest son was on national television on a special entitled, "Drug Abuse and Addiction in the US Armed Forces."

Five months out of treatment I met my first wife; we married six short months after meeting one another. I stayed off heroin but not booze. Since I did not recognize that a drug is a drug is a drug, I was content with continuing on with my alcohol consumption just as I was before going to treatment.

In the four years that followed we had two sons, and moved back and forth between the US and Germany a few times. Finally in May of 1984, I miraculously received an honorable discharge and my family and I moved back to my hometown of Renton. However, just six months later my wife wanted to return to her home in Germany; without warning or a goodbye she packed up our children and all of a sudden they were gone from my life. I continued to remain clean off of heroin, but my drinking increased immensely.

I began trade school in motorcycle mechanics and later auto body repair. It was there that I met another biker who happened to be in recovery. He suggested I go to a meeting with him, and I did. On June 21, 1986, I began my first day living completely in recovery.

I had spent the past decade in a fog, a surrealistic grey zone that can only be comprehended by those who have experienced such a haze. Now on the other side of that weather storm, I began to see things more clearly. My newfound recovery allowed me to put my energy and focus on more productive things than getting high—like my love for motorcycles. Before I got into recovery, I did not think that the world of bikers and that of those living the clean and sober life mixed, simply because I had never heard of it or had met a biker that was also clean and sober. I had been my own living example of what I thought could never mix.

I started a motorcycle club with some of the other bikers I met in meetings in late 1986. We called ourselves The Mother Fuckers, but that quickly changed to The Iron Disciples. Three years later my little club was big enough to join the ranks of a larger nationwide clean and sober motorcycle club that called themselves The Fifth Chapter.

It was during this time that I met my second wife in the fall of '87, and in 1988 my third son was born. In 1992 I made the fatal error that many of us in the program make. I quit going to meetings and stopped calling my sponsor. Shortly after I found myself working in a bar as a bouncer, disengaging myself from the support of those in the program, and it was just a matter of time before I picked up that bottle and relapsed. After getting arrested twenty-two times in ninety days of me being out on my relapse, one of my club brothers told me if I did not clean up my act he was going to break my legs. I wouldn't be able to ride with broken legs, so I entered back into the program on June 18, 1993.

In 1993, one of what were considered the big four motorcycle clubs in the world began a clean and sober support club. I, along with fourteen of my brothers, was invited to become a member. Being members of that support club paved the way for us to become full patch holders in one of the first clean and sober chapters of one of the big four one-percenter clubs in the world by 1998.

It has been thirty-nine years since I was at the Snake River, the scene that started it all for me. I have been clean off of heroin since 1978, and I haven't taken a drink since 1993. I have been a member of a clean and sober chapter in a one-percenter motorcycle club for nearly thirteen years now.

While the road has not always been as smooth as a newly-paved highway, it certainly has been a great adventure. I married and got divorced three times; I have three sons, the youngest finishing college. How many people get to say they have truly lived out their childhood dream? And I am proud to say that my three sons have never seen me anything other than clean and sober, and that has made all the difference.

SOMEWHERE ON THE ROADS through north central Montana above Helena on US Route 287 was the first place I'd ever gone over one-hundred miles per hour.

We were on that family vacation returning from Iowa on the way to Glacier National Park in our 1962 Mercury Comet station wagon with the small six-cylinder engine and three-speed automatic transmission. I begged my dad to show me what "One-Hundred Miles An Hour!" felt like. My mom forbade me from sticking my head out the open window as she nervously darted her eyes back and forth between the speedometer and my dad's face, her hand tightly gripping his shoulder as he brought the needle up into the triple digits. I held my arm, instead of my face, out the window, feeling the force of the rushing wind in my open palm. I understood then what Chuck Yeager felt when he first broke the sound barrier. I was in heaven.

Now, forty-some years later, on the same roads, I kept my speedometer at around eighty, which meant I was probably doing something closer to seventy—most motorcycles' speedometers are calibrated by the factory to read about 10 percent optimistic. Whatever my speed actually was, it felt right and I was enjoying the ride through the rolling hills on a cool morning. Golden wheat covered the prairie. Pine trees stood green and tall on the hills that were too steep for crops. Mingled among the evergreens were odd-shaped patches of brown—the skeletal remains of trees killed by an infestation of Mountain Pine Beetles that have been decimating forests all across the West in recent years. I'm sure the local farmers and ranchers hate the sight of those dead trees, but to someone just passing through, just paying attention to the aesthetics, the occasional sections of brown provide a pleasing contrast to the endless golds and greens under Montana's big blue sky.

I stopped on the shoulder and walked over a slight rise to where I couldn't see the road or my bike—I couldn't see anything that was made by man, or hear anything either. There was no wind rustling the grain in the fields, no traffic on the highway behind me, no airplanes in the sky above me; once water stopped splashing off the rock in front of my feet it was so quiet I had to take out my earplugs to hear how overpowering true silence can be.

In the far distance in every direction, rugged mountains and high ridgelines marked a boundary, creating a definable space within the vastness of a larger land around me. And the sky curved down, encapsulating me and the land I could see, and the land beyond that. I felt strangely calm and peaceful and complete standing in that golden field under the bright, unbroken blue sky knowing there was always something great and large on other side of the limits of my vision.

Then a big, white Fed-Ex truck roared past on the highway, breaking the spell. I returned to my bike, climbed on, and followed after it.

On this journey of mine—not the bike trip but my personal journey out from the damage from my childhood—I'm seeking to regain some part of myself that got lost along the way. I'm on a journey of recovery.

Recovery is hard to define here. When I first got involved with twelve-step programs many years ago it was simple: recovery meant to stop getting high and learn how to live without drugs and alcohol. The concept was easy, even though it was the hardest thing I'd ever done up to that time. Now my objective is much more subtle and elusive. I'm working to rid myself of all the negative bullshit I grew up believing about myself, that cumbersome ball and chain that keeps me from running free. A big part of me says I should just be able to forget about the past and get on with my life. *Why am I, in my mid-fifties, being haunted by things from so long ago...things I cannot change?* That's the same voice that told me so many years ago to just be strong and don't drink, don't drug. But the disease was stronger than my desire to stop and I couldn't quit until I found a fellowship to walk with me through my recovery. And now, with another related fellowship, I'm finally learning to stride away from that old, painful burden.

Walking around with lifelong feelings of insecurieriority (you won't find that word in your Funk & Wagnalls) makes for a lonely, alienating, and frustrating life. About the only time I feel secure and in control of myself is when I'm alone on my motorcycle.

I've had to start this adventure with a long, hard, objective look at my young life starting with all the painful shit. But, as hard as it is to keep from getting stuck on the negative stuff, I'm working to look past that and acknowledge the good parts also.

Experience has taught me how to do that riding on my bike. Any successful rider knows the danger of object fixation. A rider will always steer toward what he's looking at, and usually hit it. So many bike wrecks happen because something alongside the road spooks a rider. He stares at it and rides straight into it even when he had all the room in the world to maneuver past.

This often happens in curves when a rider goes in a little too fast and gets scared that he won't make it through without crashing. So he fixates on what he most wants to avoid: a tree, a sign, a pothole, a road gator, a ditch, something off the side of the road—anything but the road ahead of his wheel—and the story in the next day's newspaper states that a motorcyclist hit the only take-your-pick in ten miles on that stretch of road. Ninety-nine-percent of the time those crashes would have been avoided if the rider had trained himself to look at where he wanted to go instead of at what he wanted to miss. Looking beyond the problem allows the rider to go past safely and comfortably. It's a learned technique.

I'm learning to incorporate that skill into my life today. When I was a kid I was always on edge. I didn't realize it until recently, but I was in constant fear while growing up. I tried to stay safe by focusing on what scared me: people who hurt me, events beyond my control, and situations I needed to avoid. I never figured out how to navigate past those obstacles without running straight into them at full speed. And I've been repeating that behavior on some deep, unconscious level all my life.

And now, finally, I'm looking past the old, useless lessons of my youth to focus further down the road on the life I want to travel through for my remaining days.

Remembering the joy I felt while watching the speedometer on my parent's car hit the "ton," seeing that even a damaged landscape can be beautiful, and knowing that when I can sequester myself, turn off the noise, and look past myself, I have a chance to find another illuminated world that lies just over the horizon is a great start to that new life I'm seeking.

I stopped at the only real gas station I found on the entire trip in the town of Choteau, where Route 287 T-bones into Route 89 for the run up to Glacier. I was puzzled at myself when I realized 89 is the same highway I'd ridden out of Yellowstone the previous evening. I could have stayed on it instead of jumping on I-90 and ending up in Three Forks where I'd met my old schoolmate. If I had been paying better attention to my map I would surely have stayed on the two-laner instead of riding straight into the setting sun on the interstate. There is no reason I missed that except that sometimes coincidences have a backstory beyond rational explanation.

The white-painted gas station had a single row of three pumps out front, twin bays with cars on lifts on the left side, and a small office with a large window in the right front corner. I had to step over a sleeping dog to ask where the restrooms were. The mechanic, sitting behind a wood desk, waved his thumb and said "On the side." I should have known without asking; this was a time warp. The only thing missing was the rubber hose and double ding of a bell summoning the attendant out to fill the tank, check the oil, and wash the windshield of a '62 Mercury station wagon.

While I was filling my bike a battered pickup pulled up on the other side of my pump. The driver—a cowboy, a rancher, a farmer, I don't know which—asked me about my trip after noticing my Florida license plate. While we were talking, a guy on a small scooter rode in to fill up at the pump in front of me. He and the cowboy obviously knew each other, and they greeted each other with a few short words. The cowboy commented on the guy's scooter. "It gets me around and gets great gas mileage," said the guy as he climbed on and rode away. The cowboy spat tobacco juice onto the ground and made some derogatory comment about the little scooter. "Ah, they got their place," I said, then laughed at his reply: "Not in this state, they don't."

The ride up 89 was full of iconic images juxtaposed against modern intrusions. Old weather-beaten buildings sheltered huge immaculate tractors and other strange-looking pieces of farm equipment that I'll never understand because I didn't take the time to stop and inquire about them. I rode next to a freight train running along the highway for a number of miles. Nothing completes a mind's picture of the West like a long string of boxcars pulled by a big locomotive on a lone track passing through rural emptiness. But graffiti, elaborately spray-painted by artists—some talented, some just angry—has transformed those trains into rolling art galleries, bringing urban angst and expressionism out of the cities to the remotest reaches of America. And, in a way, it complements the countryside and adds to the beauty.

A wrong turn in the town of Kiowa took me on a twenty-four mile round-trip detour on State Highway 49, a fun, twisty road through "Open Range" to the town of East Glacier and back. I've seen open range signs before and thought they were just interesting anachronisms; this was the first time I found the range open for business. I came out of a tight, blind turn to find a big black ton of future Big Macs calmly standing in the middle of the road a short dozen bike lengths in front of me. Luckily the surface is pretty torn up and there had been a lot of gravel on the road, so I was riding relatively slow and managed to stop with room to spare. I learned later that, in the Old West tradition, branded cattle are allowed to wander freely over the land, grazing wherever they like, and have the legal right of way. If I'd hit one, I would have been responsible to the rancher for damage my bike caused to his cow.

After a quick, relaxing lunch with someone's dog curled up at my feet on the front porch at a deli in East Glacier, I returned to Route 89 at Kiowa—a town with a population of four, a resort with individual cabins for less than fifty dollars per night, and free corrals for guests who travel with their horses—and found my way north to the entrance of Glacier National Park.

I'd come to ride Going-to-the-Sun Road.

Although not as high as the Beartooth Highway, it's equally spectacular, but it is as different from the Beartooth as the Mona Lisa is from a pinup of Marilyn Monroe. The Northern Rockies are rugged and dramatic. Patches of snow survive the summer's heat in the shady recesses of sharp grey granite peaks that tower above green wooded valleys streaked with rushing whitewater rivers running down from the mountain glaciers the park is named after. The road, cut into the steep sides of the mountain's solid stone, is so tight in places that vehicles (RVs) longer than twenty-one feet or with mirrors wider than eight feet are not allowed to travel the full fifty miles of the east/west trip over the continental divide. Just west of the summit, right at the tree line below Logan Pass at sixty-six hundred feet, I stopped to watch a group of mountain goats cross the road and wander off through an alpine field. Further down the road I noticed a young Black Bear amble through a cedar forest—the more pleasant of my two bear experiences on this trip.

Leaving the park in the late afternoon at the town of West Glacier, I picked up US Route 2, which I intended to ride most of the way to Seattle.

8

I MADE IT ABOUT thirty miles from West Glacier to the city of Kalispell, Montana after leaving the park—actually, I rode quite a ways past Kalispell and turned around and went back to find a motel before stopping for the night.

One of my road rules, along with never passing up a chance to fill the gas tank, is to stop riding when it gets dark enough that I need to change the tinted face shield on my helmet to the clear shield whenever I'm in deer country. Deer come out to feed around dusk and they scare the hell out of me. From the various motorcycle groups I follow on the Internet, I probably read of a deer strike a week during the summer—and motorcycles almost always lose in those collisions. This part of Montana passes through heavy forests, prime habitat for deer, so when the sun started getting low in the sky I stopped at a local roadside market to ask if there were any campgrounds ahead of me. No one there knew for sure, so I headed back to the city after picking up a package of local buffalo jerky (bear chow) at the store.

I had a hard time finding a place that night in Kalispell. The Northwest Montana Fair was in town that week and all the places were either full or too expensive for my budget. After about a half-dozen tries I found a decent place where a lot of other riders were also staying.

Another of my road rules is never to pass up an opportunity to do a load of laundry. The motel had a small laundry room, so I threw in a load went out to talk with some of the other riders who were doing the same. Most of them were heading into Glacier, some were going south down to the Beartooth, and a few guys on Beemers were riding up to Canada for a rally sponsored by the local BMW club.

I briefly thought about trying to ride up to the rally in British Columbia. I used to spend a lot of time in BC and have crossed the border hundreds of times, but times have changed and I was afraid my past might come back to complicate my attempt to enter the country. Since 9/11, Canada and the US have opened their criminal databases to each other. I have a couple thirty-year-old DUIs on my record; I've heard Canada classifies those as felonies and frequently turns back Americans with drunk driving convictions. That is something I'll have to investigate further. Hopefully I'll be able to jump through all the necessary legal hoops and get clearance to ride through Canada; one of my future goals is to ride to Alaska and into Canada's Northwest Territories. I think because I have all this time in recovery that all that old stuff should be behind me, but it will always be a part of my life and I'll always have to deal with it on some level.

US Route 2, the northernmost highway in the national highway system, runs as parallel to the Canadian border as topography allows.

It stretches between Michigan's Upper Peninsula and the city of Everett in Washington State where it ends near Interstate 5 a couple hours north of Seattle. I'd been wanting to ride it for years and got an early start in the cold morning soon after the sun rose above the sharp mountain peaks to the east. Wearing all my gear and using the bike's heated handgrips to keep my fingers from freezing through my thin gloves, I felt frisky and set a fast mile-eating pace that lasted the entire day. The road surface was nearly flawless and the traffic almost nonexistent except for the occasional logging truck hauling timber out of the thick forest. The road was twisty and hilly enough that I'd often get caught behind these trucks for miles, breathing the scent of fresh-cut lumber while dodging pieces of bark flying off the huge trunks before finding a safe place to pass. But the morning, the road and the countryside were so perfect that even the sporadic slowdowns were more enjoyable than frustrating.

One of my hobbies is talking to strangers. I'm willing to talk with almost anyone, anywhere, just to see where the conversation will go, what I'll learn, and, when traveling, to try and discover something about the people and the places I pass through. Sometimes I'm the initiator, other times not; I'll talk politics, religion, economics, history, weather, motorcycles, medical complaints, family problems, or listen to jokes—almost anything as long as the person I'm talking to is interesting. I've learned to weed out the bores. If someone emerges from a prime panhandling spot and starts out by asking if I've ever heard of a Vincent Black Shadow, says he's going to build a chopper someday and ride across country the "right" way, or tries to convince me that my Beemer is the best motorcycle made, I get my earplugs in and helmet on real fast.

At a gas/breakfast stop in Libby, Montana, one of the parking-lot-troll variety got to me just as I climbed off my bike, so I wasn't able to pull my quick escape act. I noticed an older gentleman standing off to the side looking my bike over and I pulled him into conversation.

He asked about my bike's fuel capacity and range, commented on the wide fairing and windshield, and felt the deep padded seat before quietly mentioning he once had a Triumph he'd brought back from England after "The War." He told me he'd ridden it all over the country for twenty years before giving up riding. I showed him how I could raise and lower my windshield on the fly with the push of a button, told him about the heated handgrips, explained the sophisticated suspension, and pointed out the duel-compound tires with hard rubber in the center for upright highway runs and soft rubber on the sides for better grip while riding through curves. He told me about tearing down his engine on the side of the road—more than once—and about broken chains, faulty electrical systems, flat tires, oil leaks, and all the "charm" of riding long distances on a '40s vintage Brit bike. We spoke for the better part of an hour. I've got a lot of respect for the riding he did in his day, and I think he respects my bike for its comfort and reliability—but I know I wouldn't want to trade my bike for his and I'm sure he wouldn't want to trade his experiences for mine. We shook hands, exchanged names, and wished each other well. The troll had managed to collect enough change from passersby to get a beer and was happily back at his station by the trash bin nursing a Budweiser—he told me to ride safe; I told him to drink safe and continued on my way.

By the time I crossed into Idaho it was getting hot and I stopped to shed some gear before heading down to the town of Sandpoint, where I learned, much to my surprise, the US Navy has a submarine research center there in the high mountains of Idaho's northern panhandle. Route 2 crossed from Idaho into Washington, and I noticed the sign for Washington State Route 20.

I now have a new favorite road.

I'm familiar with the western sections of SR 20, but I'd never traveled its full length. Now I have to say it may be the most perfect road I've ever ridden. It's got everything a rider could ask for along its four-hundred-some mile length that runs from Idaho's thick mountain forest to Puget Sound near Port Townsend on Washington's Olympic Peninsula. The road can be roughly divided into six segments designated by the terrain it's passing through; it also either completely encompasses or touches on six of Washington State's own version of the Scenic Byway Program, along with two of the actual National Scenic Byways.

I turned off Route 2, which drops down south and cuts through the central part of the state, and headed north on Route 20 with the wide, gentle north-flowing Pend Oreille River on my right. This part of 20 was similar to the morning's ride; it's easy and pleasant, but a bit tighter, hillier, and curvier than Route 2 through Montana. I kept my frisky pace and made it to the tiny town of Tiger within an hour.

This second segment of Route 20 heads about one hundred fifty miles west from Tiger to the town of Tonasket in the Okanogan Valley. It's a fun and challenging ride with lots of tight switchbacks, long fast sweepers, and plenty of elevation changes. The road must have been repaved within the past couple years; its surface is almost perfect. Long stretches were open and clean with little traffic and no crossroads. I'd put lots of miles on the bike and was comfortable enough on it by then that I was able to push myself and attack the road with an aggression usually reserved for the racetrack.

Halfway between Tiger and Tonasket the highway drops down from the gentle mountains in the Colville National Forest to cross the Columbia River at the town of Kettle Falls, then climbs back up to pass over the 5,500-foot Sherman Pass before winding its way back down again to a lower elevation where it joins US Route 97 for a short thirty-mile section that runs southward through the Okanogan Valley.

Route 97 brought back fond memories of my first long motorcycle ride. Between our junior and senior years in high school, my friend Steve and I had jobs in one of the apple orchards that fill the valley along the Okanogan River. We rode his Honda 175 from Seattle over two mountain passes with all the gear we needed to live and work with leftover hippies and migrant farm workers that summer. The little bike was overloaded with the two of us, a single backpack holding our clothes, a duffle bag with an automobile eight-track tape player along with a battery charger to power it with, and a pair of speakers. We must have had a couple dozen tapes, but the only ones I remember are Graham Nash's *Songs for Beginners* and Jimi Hendrix's *Cry of Love*.

We had to stop every fifty miles on that three hundred mile ride to let the bike cool, add oil, let our butts rest, and smoke a joint. It was a great adventure for a couple of teenagers in the early seventies.

Traffic on 97 was light by city standards, but after a day of not seeing more than one or two other vehicles on the road at a time, it felt almost claustrophobic. It was a great relief when 20 broke off from 97 in the town of Okanogan and headed west to climb out of the valley's brutal heat into the mountains again. This section of Route 20 between the Okanogan and Skagit Valleys passes through the town of Winthrop before crossing over the North Cascade Mountains. The North Cascades Highway had been another road on my must-ride list; I'd driven it a few times but this was the first time I'd had the opportunity to ride it.

It was late afternoon by the time I got to Winthrop, the last town on the east side of the Cascades on the highway, and I needed food and a brief rest. I stopped in an air-conditioned pizza joint for a quick meal, made a few phone calls to some old friends and a BMW dealer in Seattle to schedule visits and an oil change for my bike, and then headed out for the town of Burlington over in the Skagit Valley.

The North Cascades Highway is similar to Going-to-the-Sun Road, but not as popular or crowded; it is equally remote and rugged, but with much less traffic. I was torn between riding hard and fast to enjoy the road or slowing down to enjoy the beauty—as usual the challenge of a twisty road won out over scenery.

Climbing the eastern side of the pass on an open section of road with the evening sun flashing out from behind the stark peaks above me, I got trapped by that beauty and felt a moment of enchantment comprised of the light, the land, and my motion and perception.

Casting long shadows down the mountainside; caught between the dark shade and bright sunshine; filtered through the green needles of the tall pine trees; bouncing off the brown trunks; and reflected off the solid grey granite, the light seemed to emit a glowing, translucent, multi-colored texture independent of its source. For a brief moment it reminded me of the northern lights— aurora borealis. But this was terrestrial not celestial. "It's arboreal borealis," I thought before clearing a tight turn and leaving it forever behind me along with my invisible tire tracks. In medieval times people would have claimed fairies lived there. It's another one of those magic moments that will always stay locked in my memory.

After clearing the 5,400-foot summit and heading down the western side I was back in direct light again for a while, but the sun was getting low in the sky and the temperatures were dropping along with it. By the time I stopped at a convenience store in Burlington to put on the second layer of my riding suit and change my gloves the sun was close to the horizon and would be setting soon, so I changed for the clear face shield on my helmet. Then I realized I might be able to make it to my favorite place on this entire planet to watch the sunset: Deception Pass Bridge.

A RUSSIAN BUILT URAL AT THE DECEPTION PASS BRIDGE

I hadn't thought about making it this far because for the most part, nothing had existed to me the entire day except the next curve in the road ahead of my front tire; I'd been living in the moment all day long with nothing more important than finding the perfect line through each twist and turn. I didn't realize how hard I'd been working until I got on the short, crowded, multi-lane freeway-like section of 20 that runs from Burlington to the turnoff leading to Deception Pass and Whidbey Island. For the first time in my life, my throttle hand's forearm was sore and achy from constantly modulating the throttle and grabbing the front brake an incalculable number of times. Racers call it arm pump, and every twist of the wrist caused a strong, dull hurt in my arm.

But it didn't slow me down. I was in a hurry now and attacked the heavy traffic with an aggression equal to that I'd been directing toward the road for the past five hundred miles. Using thirty-five years of riding skills, keeping the RPMs high in the powerband so I could easily accelerate into any gap that opened up between cars, and trusting my karma to keep cops occupied elsewhere, I put as much traffic behind me as quickly as I could and got to the bridge with the bright yellow-orange sun just a couple fingers above the horizon.

Whidbey Island has always been an important part of my life. My grandparents settled there and built a house the year I was born. I've been traveling this section of Route 20 all my life, and the curvy road, carved out of dense forest and lined with tree-trunk guardrails running to the picturesque thirties-era arched bridge, always takes me to a special place. I parked the bike on the Whidbey side and

THE BEST SUNSETS IN THE WORLD: DECEPTION PASS BRIDGE

walked out onto the bridge to watch the sun that I'd seen rise up out of the Rocky Mountains in Kalispell that morning disappear into the Pacific Ocean.

I could blame the tears that streamed down my cheeks on the cold wind stinging my eyes—but that would be a lie. A few other people came out onto the bridge but got quickly blown back into their warm cars by the blustery wind; I was alone with my thoughts and emotions. Leaning against the railing, I watched a small fishing boat round a headland and make its way through the dark, swirling water a couple hundred feet below me, no doubt heading to port in the protected waters of a secluded bay to the east of the pass. I probably had a bit of an endorphin high from riding so hard all day, and that, along with the beauty of the moment overwhelmed me with a sense of peace I hadn't felt in years. Speaking to the sun as it dropped behind the faint outline of the Olympic Peninsula, barely discernable as a low, distant silhouette in the twilight, I silently, gratefully, mouthed the words, "Thank you God for getting me here."

I don't know how to define God—I use that term because it's understood. The Power of the Universe might be the most apt description, but I have a connection, a spiritual connection, to something eternal and essential that I can almost always tap into to balance out against the heaviest, ugliest, darkest days I've lived.

Even as a little kid growing up, being scared all the time and feeling so unlovable, so defective, and so hated that I would hurt myself physically, I could walk outside at night, look up at the stars and find comfort and understand that I had value. Standing on the bridge I recognized that same power, that same God that I first felt as a scared little kid decades ago.

When I first got into recovery I used that God to help me endure the agony of living without the drugs I'd depended on for so many years. And throughout my recovery I could depend on that spiritual connection to get me through the rough times. But about eight years ago I got lost in an ugly downward spiral that conjured all those old childhood hurts up to the surface, and I couldn't cope with the adult stuff anymore either; I lost my connection to my God. My life felt uglier than I could ever imagine, and I don't know how I survived except that God must have been working for me even though I couldn't feel it.

When my friend Vivian introduced me to my current path of recovery I found a twelve-step fellowship of others who know and understand what I'd gone through and what I was going through as an adult; I began to try to reconnect with that God of my understanding.

One of the more important things I heard at a meeting was when someone said, "If your God stops working for you, go back and build a stronger God."

That's where I'm at in my spiritual path today—building a stronger God. I realize I've always used God as a way to cope with the painful things that happened in my life. Today I'm searching for a preemptive God, one who will help me build a life that doesn't involve coping. A God that I don't look for outside of myself for strength, but one that I feel from the inside out. And that's not easy. If it were we wouldn't need hundreds of religions and thousands of cults in the world—everyone would be walking around, floating a foot above the ground with an eternal smile on their face and a heavenly glow emanating from their eyes. So now I'm working hard, searching for that God who will travel with me for the next stage of my journey.

I think I briefly met that God on Deception Pass Bridge after a perfect day's ride.

9

A FLOCK OF SEAGULLS woke me with their perpetual argument over who can screech the loudest; a stiff breeze brought me the soft sounds and scents of low-tide waves breaking against the driftwood-strewn beach as I snuggled in my warm sleeping bag breathing in the cold, thick predawn air. I looked out the small window in my tent and saw low dark gray clouds scudding overhead in the lightening sky. Someone could have kidnapped me from anywhere in the world, knocked me out, and transported me here and I believe I would have, immediately upon regaining consciousness and even without seeing my surroundings, known I was in Oak Harbor.

I've witnessed the city grow from a little seaside town with a population of twenty-seven hundred into a small city with a population almost ten times that. As a kid I remember how excited my grandparents were when a name-brand grocery store finally opened and how they thought Oak Harbor was finally "on the map" when the first fast food franchise—Kentucky Fried Chicken—came to town. Then came convenience stores, more fast food, twenty-four hour gas stations, and all the trappings of the late Twentieth Century.

More recently, I recall the town unsuccessfully fighting to keep Walmart out. Now they've got a Home Depot too, and three Starbucks.

But I still love the place and hope to return there to live someday.

It was late, well after dark, before I rolled into the campground at City Beach off the corner of Route 20 and Pioneer Way. After setting my tent up by feel and familiarity, I walked across the highway to the DK Market, a tiny store I've known for more than a half century, and bought a large cup of hot chocolate brewed from an automated machine and a stale pastry to suffice as dinner. My hunger for nostalgia was greater than my need for nourishment.

I'd checked to see if the hot water worked in the campground's showers before turning in for the night, but the buildings were locked tight in the early morning; this was the first time in two weeks on the road that I'd be a genuine dirty biker for the day.

With three Starbucks stores along a mile-long stretch of Route 20, finding a place to wait for the city to wake up wasn't a problem. I got my caffeine fix, caught up on email, read the local paper, and then hit some secondhand stores for supplies. It had been three years since I'd last been in Oak Harbor, and I was sure no one had visited my grandparents' grave since then; I picked up some stuff to clean their headstone and trim the grass around it, and found an appropriate token to leave behind.

After visiting the cemetery, I rode through town and around the area looking at things both familiar and new, walked along the waterfront, and went into a bank where I still have an account. I didn't need any cash, but wanted to walk into the building and do a bit of banking the old fashioned way—face-to-face with a friendly teller who took the time to share in some pleasant conversation. The bank has changed hands and is now part of a national chain, but it was nice walking into the same building I'd followed my grandmother into years ago and doing business the same way she had.

Riding out of town, I turned off Route 20 onto Scenic Heights Road and followed the coastal route past Grandma and Grandpa's old house. It's a modest, mid-fifties place on a high bluff with a million-dollar view looking out over the water and the town, with Mount Baker and the Cascade Mountains to the north and east. On clear days, in the far distance to the south, the snowcapped dome of Mount Rainier can be seen floating, reassuringly, above the horizon, prompting the expression that every person who lives in the Puget Sound area loves to hear: "The Mountain is out today." Now their old house is surrounded by larger, fancier homes, most of them owned by wealthy retirees. I didn't stop, but was happy to see it looked better than it had on my last trip, with a new roof, a fresh coat of paint, and a recently mown lawn. Continuing on, I rolled past familiar dairies and other working farms on my way to rejoining Route 20 at the tiny unincorporated community of San de Fuca—where a still-working drive-in movie theater stands.

Almost immediately after getting back on 20 I took a left onto my very first favorite road—Madrona Way.

I hadn't thought about it before, but I guess my wanderlust was passed on to me from my grandparents, and my lifelong love of roads began on Whidbey Island.

All the roads on Whidbey are twisty rural two-laners running through forests, following the rugged shoreline or passing by multi-generation family farms. Route 20 and its extension, Washington State Route 525, running the full north/south length of the island, combine to form the final Scenic Byway on this long highway.

Madrona Way is a short three-mile-long detour running between San de Fuca to the town of Coupeville. It curves and twists on an undulating drive along the end of a large cove with the blue-grey water of Puget Sound and the Cascades beyond filtered through the orange-red, peeling-paper-bark trunks and branches of the native Madrona trees lining the road's edge. When I was a young kid this road seduced me. It's where I first realized good roads are for more than getting from point A to point B, and that vehicles should be more than a means of transportation. Even sitting in the backseat of the family station wagon felt good on this road. I learned the right combination of road and vehicle can transport a traveler from one state of mind to another. The first time I rode a motorcycle up to Whidbey to visit my grandparents I went out of my way to ride it before going to their house; I must have ridden it back and forth a couple dozen times before continuing. I was late for dinner and felt too silly to tell them the truth about why, but in hindsight I think they would have understood.

They both had the wanderlust, enjoyed adventure, and were always driving to some remote lake or National Park to go fishing or camping; the destinations, I now know, were merely excuses for a trip. They both seemed to understand and approve of my obsession with motorcycles too.

As a young man in the 1920s, my grandfather rode a Harley from Minnesota to Alaska. He eventually got hurt in a crash, sold the bike, and never rode again, but he'd keep me spellbound with his stories whenever I could get him to talk about that trip. And I once took my grandmother, who was well into her seventies at the time, for a ride on my little Honda 360. It was her first and only motorcycle ride; she had me take her by all her friends' homes so they could see her on the back of my bike. She was a giggly happy lady that day.

MY GRANDFATHER ON HIS HARLEY IN THE 1920S

Her body was failing the last time I visited her—she was in a nursing home—but her mind and memory were still sharp. It was a few months after my grandfather had passed and the only thing she wanted to do was to join her husband in heaven. She'd always been a powerful woman who was in complete control of her own life, and she had decided her future would be brief. We didn't speak of that even though it was silently acknowledged. There really wasn't any sadness in it either. What was sad was how she couldn't forget the pain of her early life; she'd go off on long, detailed, bitter rants about her childhood and how badly people, including my mother, had hurt her.

The easiest way to cheer her up was to get her to talk about her travels around the country with my grandfather. Her face would still light up with a girlish smile and her eyes would glow in joyful remembrance as she recounted road trips with no more purpose than bringing a squiggly line on a map to life by feeding it a thin layer of rubber from their Oldsmobile's tires, letting the pavement breathe the car's exhaust, and learning its story of that particular day.

I guess if I had to define what I mean when I write about recovery, about what I want to ultimately gain by working the twelve-step program I'm in today, about what I hope for myself—it'd be that when I reach the point where there isn't much road left in front of my headlight, I don't only see the painful parts of my childhood in my rearview mirrors, that I'm able to look back without any bitterness and see the roads and paths that took me to beautiful places, have memories of great adventures and experiences, and keep all the painful shit as an aside.

In Coupeville, a small town originally settled by sea captains whose ornate Victorian mansions line the streets on the hill above Penn Cove, I ate the most expensive and best meal of the entire trip in a local hangout called Toby's Tavern, mounted on a high bluff

STOPPING FOR LUNCH AND ICE CREAM IN COUPEVILLE

along the historic waterfront. I was rude and took the biggest booth in the place all for myself during the lunch rush so I could sit by a large window overlooking my sentimental homeland. For lunch I ordered a large bucket of steamed Penn Cove mussels, freshly fished out of the water I was gazing at, with homemade garlic bread to soak up the sauce and a nonalcoholic beer—all for twenty bucks, tip included.

After an ice cream cone for dessert from a place across the street from the restaurant, I hit Route 20 again and rode to the Keystone ferry terminal on the west side of Whidbey about halfway between Deception Pass and the south end of the island. To ride the remaining sixteen miles of 20 I would have had to take the ferry across to Port Townsend on the Olympic Peninsula; I was tempted, but I was eager to get to Seattle and that would have added four or five hours to my day, so I turned onto Route 525 for the ride down to the town of Clinton where I caught that ferry for the half hour voyage to the mainland.

The long line to board the ferry stretched for at least a quarter mile before the tollbooths, but motorcycles are allowed ride to the front of the line and are first on/first off (finally, the respect we deserve!). I bypassed the traffic, paid the minimal fee, got waved to the head of the staging area, and took my motorcycle for a boat ride.

10

HEADING SOUTH ON WASHINGTON State Route 99 after rolling off the ferry in Mukilteo was like getting a blast of cold water in the middle of a hot, relaxing shower because of some inconsiderate fool flushing a toilet somewhere in the house—it was a rude, shocking jolt.

I had put six thousand miles on the bike and ridden through seventeen states in the two weeks I'd been on the road. The worst traffic I'd ridden through had really only been a couple short annoyances, but this was real congestion—heavy-duty, stop-and-crawl urban traffic with no flow or rhythm. The crowded, multi-lane streets and hurried pace of aggressive big-city commuting overwhelmed me.

After so much open road through quiet country this felt like a loud, noisy trap I needed to quickly escape from. But I had traveled here for a reason. I planned on spending a couple days in Seattle.

An old friend had offered his couch for me to crash on; I was to meet him later that evening when he got off work at eight, which gave me most of the afternoon and evening to explore around my city.

It's been thirty years since I moved from Seattle, but I had come to visit at least once a year before my little sister passed away in 2004. My parents sold their house and moved to Oregon to be near my younger sister and her kids a few years ago, and I needed to look at my old home and confront memories that still live there.

Jumping onto the interstate, I rode past familiar landmarks toward my own personal ground zero. The overcast I'd woken up to in Oak Harbor had broken and the low gray clouds parted: the Space Needle stood, alone, proud and tall, against the clear blue sky on my right; then the cluster of high-rises marked the downtown area around Pioneer Square, Pike Place Market, and the waterfront; next came the baseball and football stadiums down near the Port of Seattle; and finally, close along the west edge of I-5, the historic Rainier Brewery building, where Rainier Beer ("Vitamin R" as we called it when I lived there) had been brewed. It was weird to see a new "T" for Tully's Coffee replacing Rainier's old "R" on top of the building—officially proclaiming that my old hometown had followed my lead by displacing beer with fancy caffeine-based beverages. Ahead, in the far distance to the south, with its snow-covered peak looking like it was hanging from the sky, Mount Rainier came out to welcome me home.

With the public landmarks behind me and thousands of memory-marks ahead, I took a familiar exit off the freeway toward the neighborhood where I grew up and rode straight to the short dead-end street where my childhood home stands.

I stopped and sat on my bike for a long time studying the house that I still think of as home; it's a cliché, but the house looked much smaller than I remembered.

It was deserted. The new owners had apparently abandoned it for some reason or another. The once meticulously maintained lawn was in shambles; the grass stood taller than my knees, brown and dead in the dry summer heat. Untrimmed shrubbery hung over the sidewalks, and thick patches of weeds, blocking access to the detached garage my dad built, grew through the driveway. The only thing that still looked healthy was a maple tree in the backyard that I faintly recall my dad bringing home as a spindly sapling. I remember him carrying it around the house with the thin trunk resting against his shoulder and the small bundle of roots cradled in his hand, like a soldier carrying a rifle; now its trunk is probably three feet thick and it towers close to a hundred feet above the house and garage. He eventually grew to hate that tree, complaining about the leaves he had to clean out of the gutters and off the lawn every fall; he wanted to have it cut down, but my mother wouldn't let him. I don't know if either of them really had strong feelings one way or the other about it or if it was just a power play between them. I think it's a beautiful tree.

Leaving the bike parked in the street I walked into the yard and around the house. Peering through the undraped windows I felt a strange, sad detachment from the place. Even though it might have looked good on the outside, inside was full of turmoil. I realized I never felt safe there. I suppose I wanted to be overwhelmed with emotions I could exercise, or have one of those magic movie moments where I come to some great personal epiphany that would allow me to immediately ride away into a new life—as a new man. But none of that happened. The demons didn't live there anymore; if there were any there it was because they'd followed me like long streamers floating in the air behind me from a large cobweb I'd walked through and hadn't brushed off yet.

A part of me rebels against terms like "dysfunctional family," "inner-child," and "re-parenting." They sound too much like new-age psychobabble. But I once also resisted accepting addiction as a disease, and surrendering to the disease would give me the only power I'll ever have to keep that self-destructive side of myself under control. Now I know that surrender is the foundation to my recovery from a life of substance abuse. And I accept there is still a wounded little child in me, and that I can reach inside and give him the healthy nurturing he never felt as a kid growing up and begin to recover from decades-old hurts.

The healing process involves reliving some of the old pain to understand its source and putting it all in perspective. We were a typical baby-boomer generation family in the mid-sixties. Dad worked; mom stayed home to take care of the kids, keep the house clean, and have dinner ready at six. My sister and I walked to the red-brick schoolhouse down at the end of the street. There was even a section of white picket fence standing between my mother's rose bed and a neighbor's driveway.

Walking around the house I was just an outside observer of long-ago events, like a soldier returning to an old battle site from his youth. I could remember things that happened, but not feel them. I was not able to reach in and save the little boy I was—I can only work on healing the adult I've become. Every family assigns roles to the children. My younger sister, who was one grade behind me in school, was the family hero; everything she did was perfect and praised. My little sister, who had Down syndrome, was the family mascot; everything revolved around her needs. I was the family scapegoat; everything that went wrong was my fault. It wasn't my behavior that was criticized, it was me. It wasn't the things I did that were wrong, it was me that was wrong. And the punishments were brutal, personal, cutting, and permanent; the tools of punishment were criticism, belittlement, shame, guilt, disapproval, humiliation, abandonment, and rejection.

I remember, as a preteen, hiding in my closet or under my bed from my father's anger because I was going to get punished for something, when I often had no idea what I had done wrong. Sometimes I'd get punished for things before I'd had a chance to do anything. I couldn't tell my mother how I felt about anything because whatever I felt or thought would be discounted as the wrong thing to feel or think. And I felt utterly inferior to my perfect sister. I was often in so much emotional pain that hurting myself—biting myself, hitting myself, banging my head against the wall or floor, and frequent thoughts of suicide—gave me the only relief I could find.

Not having a sound foundation to launch myself from, I never felt I was standing on solid ground. I can't remember ever feeling confident or comfortable around other people. I've never been sure enough of myself to trust my feelings or able to trust other people. I guess I have to admit I've never known how to feel loved. I've always felt like I was a step or two out of sync with everyone around me.

Somewhere along the way as I matured, as a defense against pain and frustration, I'd built a psychic cocoon to hide in, as though I'd wrapped myself in multiple layers of bubble wrap for protection to keep anything that could hurt me out. And that worked until it didn't work any longer—but at a price. My dependence on drugs and alcohol was part of that price; but a deeper, more permanent harm was how my view of the world was blurred and muffled. Eventually I became isolated inside that emotional buffer—I couldn't keep pain out without excluding joy also. I became cold and numb. Even clean and sober I was dying bit by bit. Now I'm popping all those little protective bubbles and fighting my way out. It's loud, painful, and torturous—but it's the pain of healing, not of hurt.

Now I'm in metamorphosis. Even though I've lived a lonely, frustrating life, I'm confident that my journey is leading to a peaceful place.

I wonder what butterflies feel like when they first find their wings.

Back on the bike, I rode around the old neighborhood over the winding streets that I'd first explored on my metallic-green Schwinn Stingray bicycle with the five-speed stick shift that I played Evel Knievel on, and eventually converted into a pedal-powered chopper with long front forks and a tall sissy bar after seeing *Easy Rider*.

The area—called Skyway because it's perched on top of a high, distinct hill above Lake Washington between the cities of Renton and Seattle with a wonderful view of the Cascade Mountains and Mount Rainier—was developed in the years following World War II for returning soldiers with GI Bill money to spend on mortgages. It was a good, safe community then, a nice place to grow up in and live the post-war American Dream, but it has changed in recent years. Gangs and violence have infiltrated the once-peaceful neighborhood, and many houses stand vacant; even the school at the end of the street has been torn down and replaced with a maintenance yard for the school district's motor vehicles. Almost all the stores on the main drag have closed. A bar I used to hang out in has even been converted into a storefront gospel and revival center. After a quick ride and look around I realized there wasn't anything left to hold my interest.

I headed east down a four-lane arterial, through the city of Renton, and rode up a steep hill on another crowded arterial on the other side of town to go visit my little sister's gravesite.

I used to come to this cemetery every year back in the seventies to smoke a joint over Jimi Hendrix's headstone on the anniversary of his death. There was always a small, fluid group of fans to commiserate with. It was almost a religious thing for a temporary fellowship of admirers; the first visitors of the day had to search for the simple flat grave marker in the back row next to a gravel path with nothing but Jimi's name and an etching of a guitar to mark the spot, then everyone else showing up that day just had to look for a small group of stoners standing together, usually in a cold rain, to find it.

Now there is a large pagoda-type memorial in the middle of a paved circular drive near the main entrance of the cemetery where Jimi was moved to a few years ago. A constant flow of middle-aged ex-stoners, their children and grandkids, new stoners of all ages, and regular music fans from all over the world come to visit. They can get out of the weather and rest inside the open-air building on benches while parroting the comments we first spoke almost forty years ago.

I rolled past Hendrix and went straight to the spot where my little sister's ashes are buried. After pulling some weeds and clearing a couple handfuls of dead leaves from around her marker I settled down on the grass and let my mind and emotions wander.

I've been asked by a couple different therapists and some people in my current fellowship, with whom I've shared the details from my youth, how I managed to keep from turning into a complete psychopath.

There are a couple facets to the answer to that question.

First of all, I always had that connection to a God of my understanding where I found the internal strength to cope through whatever immediate crisis I was experiencing. My ability to connect with that spiritual core of myself allowed me to find a comfort that didn't exist outside me and helped me form boundaries, philosophies, and understandings that kept me from going off the deep end. I may have teetered on the edge at times—I've certainly made plenty of mistakes—but I was always able to pull back and find the strength to stay on a path I'm mostly proud of.

Second, despite how misguided and harmful their actions toward me were, my parents are not evil, and I was always able to know that. They are good people and set a good example. Unfortunately, they did not have enough confidence in themselves to let me follow their lead on a path of my own making.

Everything I did was wrong to them. My normal childhood mistakes were moral failings in their eyes, and my AD/HD and dyslexic behaviors were interpreted as willful disobedience. Nothing I did or said ever convinced them I was trying to be "good." What started out as discipline when I was a kid turned into open hostility by the time I entered high school. I wasn't allowed to join clubs I wanted. I wasn't allowed to get a job. When I found a Montessori-type program at school I was interested in and might have done well in, my dad's comment was, "You only want to do that because you're lazy," and he wouldn't let me pursue it. He often told me how my friends didn't like me and didn't want me around.

My mother's animosity toward me grew so great that she blamed me for driving her and my father apart and told me it was my fault she had an affair with our next-door neighbor. I'd accidentally caught them together and carried that secret for two years before blowing up one day and exposing her to my dad. After that things got so bad between us and her attacks were so comprehensive that the principal at my school called me aside one day to ask me what was wrong with her and why she kept trying to get me and my friends kicked out of school.

By that time I was so withdrawn and introverted that, for a couple years during my junior and senior years in high school, I could barely put a sentence together. I was so defensive and timid that I wasn't capable of any social interaction beyond discussing drugs, rock and roll, and the next party. My only goal was to stay as high as possible so people would leave me alone.

It was such a lonely, painful time that I don't know how I survived—except for a tenuous belief in myself, a strength I didn't know I had, and an understanding that my parents were wrong and shouldn't have treated me the way they did. That belief, strength, and understanding could have only come from what I now call God.

But, just as any kid who is denied an essential element during their childhood—proper food, an education, or in my case acceptance, validation, and support—I've carried a lifelong, festering emotional wound from those days and never broke free from that influence.

It wasn't until after my little sister's death that I was able to take an objective look at my family's dynamics. My wife and I had flown into Seattle the morning my sister died from a brain tumor that had only been diagnosed a couple days prior. We were there at the hospital along with my other younger sister and parents. I was holding her hand when she took her last breath. It was sudden and devastating for all of us. Later that week, when my parents discussed her funeral arrangements, I told them I had to fly home but I'd be back for the service. I scheduled my flight home, and then they changed the date to the time they knew I'd be in Miami. At first I just accepted that they didn't want me there and I didn't say anything; that was the kind of thing I was used to. But, with time, over the next year or so, I began to realize just how wrong, how dysfunctional that was, and I understood that they either didn't listen to what I'd said, didn't believe what I'd said, or didn't care about what I needed because it wasn't what they wanted.

Then I began to realize how wrong, how dysfunctional my childhood and teen years had been, and I understood that they had never listened to what I said, didn't believe what I said, or didn't care about what I needed because it wasn't what they wanted.

And then I got mad. I began to feel sorry for myself. I got depressed. I began to feel like a victim. I wallowed in self-pity. I fell apart, and my internal world got very ugly for a number of years.

That was all part of the process I had to go through before I could begin to seek a way back out of that dark, destructive vortex and start to build my life again—but this time with a solid foundation of my own design.

Spending time in Seattle gave me a chance to take a good hard objective look at where and how I developed my sense of self—to look at how my life has evolved and picture it as a continuing story of interrelated events and influences instead of a frustrating series of punishments and put-downs.

With that knowledge I'm now able to take an inventory of what my parents did—and of what I did—right and what we did wrong. And I can, with time, effort, and help from others on the same path, discard the negatives and reinforce the positives to become the person I've always known I am but didn't know how to be.

That's part of my recovery today. It's a turning point on my journey.

I don't know how long I sat there at my sister's gravesite. I just stayed quiet and still and let myself feel and absorb whatever came up. The late afternoon shadows had stretched long and dark across the thick, manicured grass by the time I got to my feet again. I kissed the bronze plaque that holds her name, left a token, and, looking past the old obstacles, got back into motion.

Pulling into the thick, late afternoon rush-hour traffic with a few hours before I was to meet my friend Ray, I wanted to call him, bail out, and head on down the road; I'd accomplished what I came to do and needed some road time to process my thoughts and emotions, but I had an appointment to get the oil changed on my bike the next afternoon so I had to stick around.

Back in Renton I rode past some more memory traps: my old high school, The Melrose Tavern where I worked as a bartender the year before leaving town, an old girlfriend's place, and the house Ray and I shared before someone lit it on fire to cover his tracks after ripping us off for a bunch of drugs. Ray and I had been friends since junior high school, and he's the only old friend I've kept in contact with who is in recovery. When I told him about running into Sheldon at the campground in Montana, he remembered we'd all been at a meeting together at a clubhouse in Renton back in 1986.

Ray lives near the north end of Lake Washington, which gave me a great excuse to ride my favorite Seattle-area drive along the western shore of Lake Washington from Renton to the University District. Beginning as a main arterial next to the municipal airport by the Boeing airplane factory on the south end of the lake, the route hugs the shoreline through a number of expensive residential neighborhoods and lakeside parks with views of Mercer Island, two of the area's floating bridges, the Cascades, and on clear days, which this had turned out to be, Mount Baker in the far distance, before passing through the University of Washington's Arboretum and Botanical Gardens, and finally ending near the university. A diverse and eclectic collection of shops, restaurants, and interesting people who look like kindred spirits of those I'd seen hanging out in Asheville gave me a place to grab dinner at a cheap noodle shop and reflect on the day that had begun with an overcast daybreak at a cold beachside campground in Oak Harbor.

I still remembered most of the roads around Seattle, but had to depend on my phone's map program to find Ray's business in a new industrial park in a recently developed area, and then I followed him to his home further north and east near the foothills of the Cascades. We stayed up late talking about new and old stuff, filling each other in on news of friends we keep in touch with, and reliving weird and wild stories from our partying days.

RAY

I got into recovery in May of 1986. In my newfound life everything was both challenging and exciting. Having tried this in 1981 with little success, I knew I had to make some life-changing decisions. First of all, besides finding a sponsor, I also had to find a social life. Being a social person, I know now that this was one of my biggest downfalls in 1981—hanging out with the same old crowd.

In early recovery it was easy to stay both focused and involved. You listen to your sponsor, take directions, and do what he says; you're like a puppy being led around and trained. After two years I got the traveling bug. I went to Florida, Hawaii, and California—warm states, fun-in-the-sun places, girls in bikinis. But after a while even that wore thin (not the bikinis), but traveling so much.

It was the beginning of the summer of 1989 when I found myself in need of something new to stimulate me, to get the adrenaline pumping. One day my sponsor picked up a Harley from someone who was down on his luck and needed some fast cash. The fun he was having with this bike was incredible. He told me, "You know Ray, you should get a bike." I said, "I would, Larry, but I've never ridden a bike before. I've known a few people who have bought new bikes and dumped them before they ever got out onto the street." "Well," Larry said "there is a safety course you can take that will teach you how to ride. Did you know if buy a new bike from a dealer, they will pay for that course?"

In the summer of 1989 I rode my first motorcycle and haven't looked back since. At first it took all my concentration to do anything on that bike; I always rode with an experienced rider along with me, out of the fear of riding alone. As time progressed I started venturing out more on my own. This is when riding started to become really enjoyable for me. I could ride at my own pace, fast or slow, safe or unsafe—the decisions were mine. I remember riding up to Mount Rainier National Park alone for the first time, and how peaceful and serene it was.

After a while I started riding with groups of people in recovery. This is when my riding became part of my recovery. I got involved with going on toy runs, poker runs, and campouts. The meetings at those campouts were incredible. There is something about a campfire and recovery that work well together. Those meetings were more about solutions than others I have attended.

In 1995 I got married and sold my bike. My recovery seemed to backpedal at that point; things were not the same. I missed the bond I had with others who shared the need to ride. Away from my biker friends, I felt like I was in a trap with people who were more concerned about possessions than recovery, as if people were measuring their and others' recovery by the material possessions they had. This moved me further and further away from my recovery.

In 2001 I got divorced. This threw me back into recovery full-bore. Things were about the same as when I left—most of the people had changed, but not the situations. It still seemed as though people based their recovery on material positions. That May I decided for my fifteen-year recovery anniversary I would buy myself a gift and—surprise, surprise—it happened to be a bike. What a difference. I found a group of people in recovery to ride with, and almost immediately my life changed.

We were kind of a home group on wheels. Every Saturday we would pick a new meeting to ride to. If someone from the group was missing, we would get a hold of them and make sure everything was all right before we headed out. Some days our group would be up to thirty bikes. Without fail, we would always pick up another biker or two at the meeting to go out to dinner or coffee with us.

In 2008 I got involved in another relationship. This time I met someone who loved to ride on the back of my bike, and she understood my need to ride alone and with the group too. After riding with me a while, she and I decided to get a bigger bike. Now with a bagger we could go on longer trips and be more comfortable, something I could do alone before, but now we could do together.

Recently a close friend in recovery lost his life on his bike. I considered this guy to be one of the safest, most knowledgeable riders I knew. He rode almost every day of the ten-plus years I had the pleasure of knowing him. The accident was the weekend before his daughter's wedding; it was Father's Day weekend and his fifty-eighth birthday. This scared me off my bike for a while. What if that happened to me? What would happen to my family? I saw what it did to his.

My first thought was that it was time to sell my bike. And I think I had decided that is what I was going to do, but when I attended his funeral and was around hundreds of people in recovery, most on bikes, my outlook started to change. I know in my heart that this wasn't something he would want. I know he would want me to keep riding with the group and to keep riding a part of my recovery.

A late start the next morning gave me just enough time to make my appointment at the local BMW dealership. I normally do all the maintenance on my bikes myself; it was time to check the valves and change the oil. The valves are easy—an hour or so in the morning before breaking camp while the bike was cold would take care of that, but oil and filter changes can be messy, and finding a place to dump used oil can be a problem. It's simpler to pay the money and let the pros take care of it.

While waiting at a coffee shop near the Beemer shop, my friend Steve—from that first long motorcycle ride up the Okanogan Valley—called. Steve, Ray, and I had all been buddies "back in the day" and had all used the same way. Ray and I ended up in recovery, but Steve had just quit when he realized it was time to mature and get serious about life. He doesn't ride anymore either, although he built a custom chopper that's brought home a number of trophies from the show circuit. We got together for dinner and I ended up crashing at his place.

In the morning I pointed my front wheel east and began meandering my way back home.

RAY TOLD ME ABOUT a local clean and sober motorcycle club, the Alky Angels MC, that was hosting a campout east of the mountains near the city of Yakima. I needed to balance the negativity I'd let myself indulge in while visiting Seattle with some positive energy, and there's a great road running over the Cascades that leads straight from Renton to the rally site. Yakima sounded like a good destination.

A fast ride south down I-5 back to and through Renton in the light Saturday morning traffic put me on a local road that led through familiar country filled with small family farms and tiny towns before tying into Washington State Route 410 in the city of Enumclaw.

Route 410 between Enumclaw and the town of Naches—a town just west of Yakima and the actual site of the campout—is another National Scenic Byway. The road was originally a trail for ox-drawn wagons crossing the Cascade Mountains back in the mid-1800s; the "modern" road was built using horse-drawn wagons in the early 1900s. Now named the Chinook Scenic Byway, it passes massive old-growth evergreens in three national forests and Mount Rainier National Park, and plays with the tree line while crossing over two passes (Chinook and Cayuse). Four different rivers run parallel to the road, two on the thickly forested western slope, and two on the dryer, harsher, more dramatic eastern side.

Just west of the summit at Chinook Pass a six-mile spur leads to Crystal Mountain Resort, where I learned how to ski. A number of bicycle racers were furiously pumping up the steep, curvy road while I merely twisted my wrist to speed past. At the base one chairlift was running up to a peak-top lodge; I thought about riding up for lunch until I learned that the single ride cost the same amount I'd paid for my first pair of skis back in the late sixties. A hot drink at the combination ticket booth/snack bar cost almost what I used to pay for day's lift ticket. The girl who served my hot chocolate wasn't really interested in my nostalgia, but listened politely as I mentioned five-dollar lift rates, wood skis, leather lace-up boots, and cable bindings—I don't think she had any idea what I was talking about.

When I first started motorcycling I rode year-round and my ski clothing was my winter riding gear; it was never warm or dry enough. Now my modern RUKKA riding suit is light and loose enough I could ski in it and be much warmer and dryer on the hills than I was back then. I became a pretty good skier in my younger years, and that was partially due to my timidity and fear of other people. I usually skied alone and was more afraid of running into someone I knew than I was of hurting myself on the hard runs that most skiers were afraid of. I had to ski well to hide out on the difficult terrain that intimidated others in order to protect my insecure inner-self.

Weird, yes, but that was my life, and looking back, there were some benefits to it.

One of the things I flashed on while visiting in Seattle was how all my friends from back then came from difficult homes. Steve moved out of his parent's house and started supporting himself at the age of sixteen. To this day I've never heard Ray mention his father; I don't know much of his family life except that he started running wild without much supervision at a very young age. Other friends had parents who were hardcore alcoholics and let us drink and get high in their homes. My first girlfriends had all been sexually abused by family members. I don't think any of us realized we might be wounded; we just seemed to belong together and drank and used drugs without wondering if there was any underlying need. I guess we were sort of a fellowship of necessity, a fellowship of coping. None of us ever talked about real stuff back then and none of us really keep in touch with each other today, except for when I call when visiting town.

I don't think I had ever traveled down the eastern side of Route 410 past the turnoff to Crystal Mountain. It's a wonderful, beautiful, fun ride equal to any of the passes I'd ridden over on my way heading west. By the time I got to Naches the elevation dropped enough and I was far enough inland that I had to remove the inner layer of my riding suit for the first time since I crossed over the North Cascades Highway into Burlington four days prior. I didn't know where the campout was so I waited at a convenience store on the edge of town until I saw a group of riders go past and followed them down a nice rural county road past apple orchards and old farms straight to the campground.

As soon as I pulled in and got off my bike a bunch of guys welcomed me and a guy named Bruce, the campout's chairperson, directed me over to the registration table where his girlfriend and co-chair Jeanette checked me in and told me the schedule for the evenings activities—dinner, followed by a group ride, and then a meeting after we returned to camp.

BRUCE

I got my first bike at twelve years old in 1969. It was a 1968 Honda 90. We lived out in the country, so my friends and I rode everywhere.

In 1971 I was introduced to prescription painkillers as a result of a near fatal motorcycle accident. After that, I was off and running in my disease. I continued riding motorcycles throughout my using and definitely have the scars to remind me. I tagged along with many different motorcycle clubs, but never joined any of them.

When I was thirty days into recovery in the spring of 1990, a bunch of guys were riding to the Seaside Convention in Oregon, so I tagged along with them. One of the guys, Greg, was a friend from my childhood whom I had ridden with. He was an Alky Angels member. We got to Seaside and I met dozens of guys from all over the Pacific Northwest who were also members of the Alky Angels. That weekend I witnessed a camaraderie that was truly amazing. These guys looked out for one another and were involved in each other's lives even when they lived hundreds of miles away from each other. They were a family. They made me feel welcome right from the start. I decided I wanted to join this club. I told my friend Greg, and he took me over to the international chairman, Ricardo, who informed me that they do not normally sign people up at thirty days in recovery. Greg and a couple other guys vouched for me and they let me join that day.

That was over twenty years ago, and I am still a member of the Alky Angels today. I plan on being a member for my lifetime.

I can remember one year, our local chapter was down to only two members and we had no idea how we were going to put on our annual campout. I made a lot of phone calls, reached out to the membership, and asked for help. The response was phenomenal. Everybody showed up ready to pitch in and work. There were a few bumps along the way (like the stew we served had raw potatoes and carrots in it), but it was one of the biggest and best campouts the Yakima Chapter ever had. It was a family coming together.

JEANETTE

I have been around motorcycles all my life. My dad was in the military, and around military bases there were always motorcycle clubs, either small local clubs or large well-known one-percent clubs. I have always been attracted to the biker lifestyle.

When I got into recovery in 1989 and met the Alky Angels, I just hung out and watched. I thought I knew what they were going to be all about, since I had grown up around bikers my whole life—contempt prior to investigation. But I was wrong.

Instead of the macho, chauvinistic attitude I was expecting, I found acceptance, understanding, and camaraderie. I was included and accepted before I ever joined.

Then I started dating Bruce, who was an Alky Angel member. For years I refused to be an associate member on his membership (my old tapes—too much like "property of" for my liking), and so I just hung around. Then I got my endorsement and a bike of my own, and I joined the club myself. My not being an "official" member had never stopped anyone from including me.

My local chapter in Yakima even elected me an officer before I joined. As they said, "You are here at every meeting, so we might as well give you a job and put you to work." I am so grateful today to be a part of such a wonderful organization. I am now in contact with some of the most fabulous people on a regular basis. We have scheduled events that are sponsored by each chapter throughout the year, and we also attend events put on by other clean and sober clubs in our area. They cover a wide range of interests—toy runs, dinners, dances, golf tourneys, meetings, and campouts, just to name a few—and you are never required to be a rider of a motorcycle to attend. We do pretty much anything we can think of to have fun, ride, and carry the message. We even put together a wallet-sized run calendar of all the clean and sober motorcycle events in our area so we can pass them out to people. We are always hoping to attract new people and show them that you don't have to drink and use to have fun riding.

The Alky Angels International was formed in 1978 and is an association rather than a club. Anyone who is in recovery and rides is welcome to join without probationary periods or initiation rituals. There are a number of Alky Angels chapters around the Pacific Northwest and they, along with a half-dozen other clean and sober clubs, host a variety of campouts, rides, charity events, and meetings almost every weekend all summer long.

My mental health and spirituality have always been connected with riding, and I am so glad to have found a group of like-minded people who share the principles of the program to guide their lives.

Well over a hundred riders were at Yakima, and I immediately felt at home among them.

My bike fell over while I was setting up my tent. I'd put it on the center stand because I knew the side stand would've sunk into the soft grass, and without any drinkers around there weren't any beer cans to stomp flat to rest it on; I've never had a bike fall

AT THE ALKY ANGELS CAMPOUT IN YAKIMA

off the center stand but there's a first time for everything. Almost before I could react a bunch of guys came running over to help me pick it up. The only damage was a broken latch on the right-side saddlebag. I tried an emergency J-B Weld repair on the cast aluminum latching piece, but that snapped as soon as I tried it in the morning. Eventually I got some double-sided tape at a local Ace Hardware store in town, and that, along with a one-liter water bottle wedged between the camping gear's duffle bag and the top of the saddlebag, held it in place for the week it took me to get back home.

Dinner was fajitas, a big huge plate of some of the most delicious fajitas I've ever eaten. I sat next to Larry, who's been a member of Alky Angels since he began riding in 1984, three years after he

LINING UP FOR A POLICE ESCORTED RIDE TO
DAIRY QUEEN WITH THE ALKY ANGELS

got into recovery. He had one of his kids, two of his grandkids, and a newborn great granddaughter camping with him that weekend—that's four generations camping and having fun together. While we were eating, a group of motorcycle cops rode into the campground and parked close to us. I figured we were in for a shakedown until someone filled me in on the traditional after-dinner ride to Yakima—the police were there to escort us.

After a quick briefing from the police, we—fifty-nine motorcycles—pulled out of the campground in staggered formation and, with six moto-cops blocking traffic from side streets and stopping cross traffic at intersections as if we were important dignitaries on official business, rode unhindered to a downtown Dairy Queen for ice cream. I giggled inside my helmet most of the way. Locals were coming out onto their front lawns cheering, clapping and waving, and smiling at each other, as a bunch of ex-drunks and ex-druggies on big, loud, menacing motorcycles, most wearing club colors, had the police clear the way for them to ride into town for after-dinner treats on a wonderful, warm, beautiful Saturday night in a small farming community in Eastern Washington. It sure is a far cry from what happened back in Hollister in 1947. It might even be close to a miracle.

12

WAITING FOR THE MORNING sun to dry the dew off my tent, I walked around talking to people, ate breakfast, and drank coffee out of the Alky Angels coffee mug I'd been given as a prize for "longest distance traveled to the rally" at the awards ceremony the night before.

I was wrestling with a dilemma. My parents and younger sister live a short three hundred miles from Yakima in Eugene, Oregon: *Do I head southwest and go visit them, or do I just aim the bike southeast and head home*? My thoughts went back and forth a dozen times; I had both routes marked on my map and considered flipping a coin but didn't—the decision was too important for chance. Finally I decided to go visit; then I decided not to go visit and felt better, so I knew that was the right way to go. I don't think I hold any animosity toward my family, but I don't think I could see them yet without that wounded little boy inside me coming out and my adult self regressing back into that unhealthy family role I was assigned so many years ago. Perhaps next year I'll feel strong enough to visit them. I hope so. I'm working on it.

In Naches, Washington SR 410 becomes US Route 12, which then joins Interstate 82 in Yakima and heads south out of Washington. I'd broken my first rule of riding that morning and passed a number of gas stations. By the time I got to a truck stop in the town of Umatilla, Oregon after crossing over the Columbia River, my fuel warning light had been flashing for many miles and I'd been expecting the bike to come to a sputtering stop any minute. I poured six-and-one-half gallons of fuel into a tank that should, according to the owner's manual, only hold one-tenth more than that.

About ten miles past the gas stop I took a left where southbound I-82 T-bones into Interstate 84. I was eastbound now and this was a day for putting on miles; I hoped to make it to Utah before stopping for the night.

I-84 rises out of the Columbia Basin into the Blue Mountains with the tightest curves of any interstate in the US. Climbing up the steep grade, another guy on a Honda decided he wanted to be my riding partner and tried to hang with me by riding in the blind spot a little behind me on the right-side tire track in my lane. This annoyed me. I'd lose him in the sweeping curves that apparently intimidated him. Oregon is notorious among the long distance riding community for strict enforcement of its artificially low speed limits, so I didn't risk keeping my speed up on the straights, and this guy would catch up and drop into formation again. I tried slowing and letting him get ahead of me, but I'd catch up as soon as we got into some curves again. When I noticed a sign for an upcoming rest area at Deadman Pass, I let him stay close until we were right at the exit then I grabbed a handful of brake and cut off behind him as he shot past. It was getting cool up in the mountains and I wanted to add another layer of clothing, so the stop wasn't a complete waste of time.

I didn't take the time to look, but I read there are still visible tracks from the wagon trains that followed the Oregon Trail over the pass back in the days when travel was measured by miles per day and the faster you could go the better; now we measure travel by miles per hour and get penalized for making too many of them in too short a time. That's progress?

While I was putting on my jacket liner another Beemer rider pulled into the space next to me. We talked for a few minutes; he was headed out to Indianapolis from Portland to watch the MotoGP motorcycle race—motorcycling's international equivalent to auto racing's Grand Prix series—the following weekend. I'd been thinking of doing the same, but didn't want to stay that far north and ride states I'd already traveled through. My plan was to ride diagonally across the country on as many two-lane back roads as I could pick out along the way. I wanted to stop in Boulder, Colorado to visit an old friend from Miami, find some fun mountain roads in Arkansas, and then meander through Alabama and Georgia on rural roads before making a final homebound run down the slab through Florida.

Back on I-84 I kept pretty close to the speed limit and made efficient time through the state with only one quick stop in Baker City to remove the jacket liner, fuel up, and wolf down a Quarter Pounder from a McDonald's across the street from the gas station. As I was leaving, the Beemer pilot I'd met at the rest stop pulled in; we nodded and kept going our separate ways.

Crossing the Snake River put me into Idaho where the highway speed limit jumped from a frustrating sixty-five up to a more satisfying seventy-five—same terrain, same roads, but a river, a political border, and different laws making an additional ten miles per hour acceptable on one side where it would be expensive on the other.

I'd been watching my clock and found a place to stop and phone in to my Sunday evening meeting, but couldn't find a good enough connection, so I missed the meeting for the first time since we'd started a step series the previous December. Passing the exit leading to Twin Falls, I thought about pulling into the city and searching for the monument commemorating Evel Knievel's failed attempt to jump his rocket–powered "Skycycle" over the Snake River Canyon in 1974, but didn't want to give up the time.

Past the city I began to smell smoke and could see a thick, dark haze to the south indicating a wildfire out on the prairie just as dusk was catching me out on the road for the first time since the ride up I-95 leaving Florida weeks before. When the sun fully set the temperature on the 3,700-foot high desert dropped and I had to stop to put on both the pants and jacket liner, and even had to use another feature of the jacket's liner. It has an air chamber that can be inflated through a tube tucked into a pocket under the collar to give an additional layer of insulation around my torso. Blowing this up, raising the windshield to the highest setting, and using the heated handgrips kept me comfortable so I could ride late enough to watch a massive, bright yellow full moon rise out of the eastern horizon directly ahead of me before I stopped for the night in the town of Burley about an hour short of Utah.

The morning coolness that comes at 4,100 feet defeated the bright morning sun's warmth, and I still needed all my gear when I pulled out of the motel soon after daybreak. Although it would get hot later, this was the lowest elevation I'd see all day. Staying on I-84 I ran down into Utah, past Ogden to where I caught Interstate 80 and ran up to Lyman, Wyoming, where I had to warm up at a truck stop and add another layer of clothes under my riding suit.

From Lyman I jumped off the interstate and headed south on Wyoming State Routes 410 and 414 into Utah, where the numbers on the same road changed to Utah State Routes 43 and 44, which joins US Route 191 to form the Flaming Gorge-Uintas National Scenic Byway.

I don't retain much memory from The Flaming Gorge, or the ride across Colorado on US Route 40. Researching it all later on the Web, I found all sorts of beautiful images that I have no recollection of; I even forgot riding over the top of the 500-foot high Flaming Gorge Dam. I do remember the terrain being beautiful and varied, the roads were fun and challenging, the scenery was spectacular, the weather was perfect, the people I met were nice, but all that comes back to me as if I'd read it in a magazine or seen it on the Travel Channel—not like firsthand experience. Maybe I was just overloaded from all the beautiful country I'd already ridden through and the emotions I'd dredged up in Seattle; I don't know. Maybe I was too focused on making it to Boulder and just didn't pay attention to my surroundings, like I was riding with blinders on.

Thinking back on what did stick with me: passing through the town of Dinosaur near the western border in Colorado sticks in my memory because we'd stopped there on one of those family vacations out to Iowa when I was a kid. I did notice quite a few freshly hit deer on the side of the road; huge tracts of dead, brown trees covered entire hillsides in some areas, killed by the Mountain Pine Beetle infestation that I'd first seen evidence of in northern Montana; and at the top of one long downhill section of Route 40, a sign announcing a 10 MPH turn at the first of a series of switchbacks with an additional sign on the post indicating there were ten more turns just like that one. That excited me until I discovered there must be some sort of mining operation near there because I kept getting stuck behind big trucks that forced me to take those turns at a frustratingly slow ten miles per hour. Somewhere along the way, probably in the Flaming Gorge area, I'd shed a couple layers of clothing because the afternoon got brutally hot, but as evening came on and I started getting caught in shadows up at nine thousand feet, the temperature dropped and I had to stop to re-layer. Also, in my haste to get to Boulder, I broke another of my rules and changed from the tinted face shield to the clear and continued riding after dark, even after seeing all that fresh roadkill during the daylight.

Finally, just a little past Winter Park, after a couple hours of watching for the reflection of glowing eyes on the side of the road while covering my brakes waiting for a deer to come bounding out of the forest in front of me, the fatigue of hyper-vigilance caught up with me and I needed to stop; I saw a sign for Robbers Roost campground and pulled in.

Reading the sign at the entrance in the glow of my headlight, I almost missed the typing-paper sized notice warning of recent bear activity in the area that was tucked into one corner of the reader board. It advised campers to lock all their food in their vehicles. *What's a motorcyclist supposed to do?* I circled the campground twice on the deep-gravel road trying to pick a spot. Only two other sites were occupied; one with a couple guys on duel-sport motorcycles, and some guy with an SUV was in another. They were both on the outer perimeter; I ended up choosing a site in the inner island-like center. The tall spruce trees blocked the light from the full moon, and it was so dark on the ground that I had to use the bike's headlight and my flashlight to set up my tent. Looking straight up through the gaps in the trees the sky absolutely glowed with the millions of twinkling stars that will eventually illuminate all the universe's secrets to us mortals here on Earth who desperately seek its knowledge. I walked to the restroom—a pair of outhouses—and noticed another sign about the bears tacked on the door.

I had a couple pounds of raw nuts, some hard candy, a few packages of freeze-dried meals, and a little of the Buffalo jerky I'd bought outside of Kalispell with me, some in the duffle bag and some in my tank bag. Usually I keep all this in the tent with me to keep it safe from animals, but squirrels and raccoons are not bears. I thought about putting it in one of the saddlebags, but decided against that. I put the tank bag and my toiletry kit in the duffle and tried to find a tree to hang it from with a length of rope I had with me, but spruce trees have short branches that are high off the ground and I couldn't reach any. Eventually I just left the duffle on the picnic table in the empty site next to mine and climbed into the tent and fell right to sleep.

I don't know if I heard him or just sensed him, but sometime during the night I woke with a bear outside my tent. I listened to his paws grind into the thick gravel as he investigated me, then heard my duffle land on the ground when he pulled it off the table and carried it off into the woods. I figured he wasn't interested in me, rolled over, and went back to sleep.

Sometime later I woke to the sound from the two riders in the site across from me starting their bikes, revving them up, and honking the horns. Soon after that the guy with the SUV started yelling and banging pots and pans together. This went on for a couple hours interrupting my sleep.

In the predawn light I got up and talked to my neighbors. The riders had left their food in the soft cloth saddlebags on their bikes that were parked right next to their tents. One guy's tent was torn where the bear kept stepping on it while ripping open the bags on his bike with his sharp claws. When the bear finished and went to the SUV guy's site is when they started their bikes in an effort to keep the bear from returning.

When I walked over to talk with the SUV guy, he was just finishing a hit from a bong; he had a freshly poured beer with a nice head on it in a schooner glass and an uncorked bottle of Jack

MY LUGGAGE AFTER THE BEAR FINISHED EATING

Daniels sitting on his picnic table. He'd left a couple coolers full of food sitting out in his site and everything edible had been eaten. His wife was so scared she wouldn't come out of the tent to meet me.

I wandered around the campground and found my bags a couple hundred feet up a slope. One of the bike guys later told me the bear was sitting about fifty feet farther up the slope watching me gather my stuff, then calmly wandered away when I had everything picked up. Somehow the bear had managed to hook the zipper-pull and open the duffle without damaging it; the tank bag had a slice, looking like it was cut with surgical precision, running parallel to and about an inch beneath the zipper, which I was able to repair with duct tape well enough to make it home.

Thinking back, I'm amazed, and a little puzzled. How I can calmly sleep when I know a hungry bear is searching for food on the other side of a thin nylon wall of my tent, but I don't have the strength to go visit my parents?

That's the dichotomy of my life, and every step of my journey is bringing those two pieces together.

13

I'M OLD-FASHIONED. I STILL drink water instead of hydrating. And on a blisteringly hot rural road in Arkansas I realized I hadn't drunk enough water that day. I was hot, thirsty, and tired, and, most disappointing, wasn't enjoying myself. It was time to stop hunting for more fun and just ride for home.

I was on US Route 71 south of Fort Smith and had just passed a thermometer on a bank reading ninety-seven degrees—combined with the thick southern humidity, that temperature could have earned a "feels like" rating of at least four-hundred-twenty-something. The convenience store I stopped at had a seating area where some locals were munching down on a healthy helping of fried chicken gizzards and other foods I didn't recognize for a mid-afternoon snack. I nursed a large Red Bull and a quart of water while absorbing the coolness from the air conditioning.

Arkansas has some of the best riding roads (although with some of the worst pavement) in the country. My friend Lourdes from Boulder, Colorado, had once lived there and helped me plan a nice ride through the state, which she'd marked with a yellow highlighter on my torn and wrinkled map. But at this point trying to keep the ride going was like forcing down a second and third plate at an all-you-can-eat Chinese buffet simply because it's there, paid for, and tasted good the first time. I recalculated a more direct route straight down Route 71 to Interstate 20 in Shreveport, Louisiana, which would take me east to where I could drop down further south to Interstate 10 and make a run for home once I hit Interstate 75 and the Florida Turnpike.

Every long ride ends sometime before the odometer records the final few hundred miles, and, with hindsight, I should have realized this one was ending when I didn't bother to stop and call a friend while passing through Denver. The road hadn't exactly become an enemy, but it wasn't as friendly as it was when home was behind my back; it wasn't a comforting companion anymore, but a worthy opponent—meant to be crushed by my tires with the pieces blown out my exhaust pipe. Miles weren't something to count, but had become something to collect. Missed turns weren't adventures, but annoying time wasters. The phone wasn't a strong enough connection to my wife's voice any longer, and my sleeping pad and a crumpled riding jacket weren't a comfortable substitute for my mattress and pillow at home. I felt like I do when traveling in a car: even though I still enjoyed the country I was traveling through, the destination had become more important than the journey.

I'd spent the day after the bear encounter with Lourdes in Boulder. We used to ride together when she lived in Miami, but she sold her Sportster a couple years ago to cover a down payment on a house in the Rockies. Although we've been good friends for many years, I don't know much of her background. She came into recovery not long after I did and got real involved with the program for a lot of years, but she's one of those whose journey eventually led her away from the rooms. It seems that some people feel threatened by those like her who can come in and get their lives in order, get healthy, develop a spiritual connection and move on, finding a workable balance between their old and new lives. I've seen a lot of people fail in that attempt—and it's not an experiment I'm willing to explore—but Lourdes seems to be one of the very few who didn't lose any of what she gained by going out of the program.

Lourdes, her partner Elaine, and I had a wonderful day together playing tourist. After breakfast at a casual local restaurant called the North Boulder Cafe—my favorite restaurant of the entire trip—we stopped at a store to replace all the foodstuff the bear had taken, then toured the Peak to Peak Highway, a Colorado State Scenic Byway and my last "destination road" of the trip. The Peak to Peak hovers around nine thousand feet, within sight of the tree line and the high, rugged, sharp edge of the Continental Divide—which I'd crossed early that morning on my way into Boulder from the campground at Robbers Roost. It was a little strange climbing in and out of a cage all day instead of on and off the bike, but it sure was easier to talk and was a nice way to spend my last day in the mountains until the next time I'm fortunate enough to make another trip out west.

Zigzagging through eastern Colorado, Kansas, and Oklahoma on a combination of Interstates 70 and 40, and a bunch of southbound two-lane US Routes, it took me a day and a half to make it to Arkansas from Boulder. I've looked down at that country through a small, rectangular, double-paned plexiglass window from thirty thousand feet way too many times. Through the boring altitude of air travel it all looks flat and empty, marked only by the occasional

WITH ELAINE AND LOURDES NEAR
THE PEAK TO PEAK NATIONAL SCENIC BYWAY

river and circular shapes dotting the land like a bunch of spots from a giant Twister game for space aliens—put your left hand on the dark green circle and your right foot on the brown one, while your opponent attempts to place her hand on the light green spot and...

From the ground, rushing past on two wheels, the Eastern Plains are still boring and empty. It truly is the wide-open spaces; it's a good place to make good time. After passing the first few farms and noticing how the efficiency of modern irrigation systems creates those round crop fields, and after getting over the fascination of seeing huge wind farms sprouting up on all the high ground, it's pretty monotonous. The interstate would have been only slightly less unbearable than flying over. At least the two-lane roads ran through small towns, many of which are just a crossroads with a grain elevator, a co-op gas station, and a grocery store. But the small towns were a diversion, especially in Kansas where every one seemed to have a museum of some sort. I don't think I ever saw one of the museums open, but they were there nevertheless.

I had to use Google to learn that a large bunch of flying butterflies can either be called a rabble or a swarm. I just call it a fucking mess when thousands of yellow-winged butterflies go on a group kamikaze mission and plaster themselves all over the front of my motorcycle. I hit a swarm near the Colorado/Kansas border and couldn't get my electric windshield raised fast enough to keep my face shield from becoming almost completely obscured by a film of yellow ex-butterfly wings. I had to raise my face shield and duck down below the windstream behind my windshield to make it to a truck stop and wash myself, the bike, and my helmet before continuing.

It was strange to think of this wide-open landscape as the new epicenter for America's alternative energy strategy. Almost every time I stopped for gas on the entire trip there was a little sticker on the pump letting me know that 10 percent of what I was pouring into my tank was ethanol—an alcohol-based fuel additive distilled from (in the US) corn. Almost all of the crops I saw along those roads would end up in someone's fuel tank instead of on a dinner table. And now, growing out of those fields, along with the ethanol-producing grains, were thousands of light grey wind turbines, each standing hundreds of feet tall with a trio of one-hundred-and-twenty-foot-long blades, turning the predictable, steady mid-American breeze into electricity to power the toys and tools we need to keep us comfortable and entertained when we aren't on the road burning through another few gallons of gas.

Heading south out of Dodge City, Kansas I got lulled into a false sense of security thinking that, because I was out of the mountains and northern forests, deer weren't a threat any longer. I'd already changed to my clear face shield, and on a beautiful, empty, straight, undulating rural road I was distracted by the bright red disc of the sun settling into the horizon on my right while, simultaneously on my left, the yellow mostly-full moon was rising into the eastern sky. I almost nailed a pair of medium-sized animals. I still don't know what they were—small deer, foxes, coyotes, dogs—whatever they were, they came out of the underbrush so suddenly and were so close that one made it across the road in front of me and the other behind. No skill, talent, or vigilance kept me upright that time; it was complete and total luck. It took me another hour of slow, watchful riding to find a motel in Woodward, Oklahoma where I stopped for the night.

The three-quarter day run through Oklahoma into Arkansas was just a long, hot, uneventful run through Oklahoma into Arkansas. The only thing that sticks in my memory was a guy on a Yamaha who, like the guy in Oregon, decided he wanted to be my riding partner. Maybe hanging with a touring bike gives these guys some sort of vicarious thrill about being out on the road themselves; I don't know, but I lost him using the same tactic I'd used at Deadman Pass.

My refigured route south down through Arkansas took me into the northeastern corner of Texas, then back to Arkansas before leading into Louisiana where I made it further south and slightly east of Shreveport on Interstate 20 before fatigue forced me to find a motel for my last stop of the trip. Even though it was dark, I wasn't worried about wildlife on the interstate, and I wanted to keep going to make the final day's run as short as possible. Sometimes it's worth it to push on through, and when I have to I can, but I needed rest and a full night's sleep was the best strategy.

14

I TOOK MY TIME loading the bike in the morning. With a little more than eleven hundred miles to go, a bit of dawdling wasn't going to make any difference to my schedule. I just wanted to stay relaxed, enjoy the day, and make it home without stopping for another night. The Weather Channel showed a tropical system moving up from the Gulf of Mexico into southern Alabama and the Florida panhandle, so I wrapped my gear in plastic for the first time since Iowa, kept the raingear handy, and headed east on I-20.

After a hundred miles or so, I stopped in a small roadside town to scarf down an Egg McMuffin and fill the tank. An older lady who was sitting at the table next to mine at McDonald's caught my attention; she was by herself and almost every one of the local "old timers" who came in greeted her with a friendly word, but left her alone. Eventually, she got up, came over, sat down at my table, and began to talk. She'd grown up in the town, married her high school sweetheart who was an engineer for the railroad, taught elementary school in the town for forty years, traveled all over the country during summer recess in the cabooses on the trains with her husband, and had recently, after sixty-three years of marriage, been widowed. She told me she was proud of her children, hated the war, was a dyed-in-the-wool liberal, and couldn't understand how her friends and neighbors supported the Bush presidency—then she wanted to know all about my trip. Where had I been? What kind of motorcycle did I ride? How long had I been on the road? What had I seen? Did I camp or stay in motels? Why did I like to travel? And on and on. It was a delightful conversation.

Originally I'd planned on heading down to I-10 on some state road in Louisiana, but I-20 was a pretty pleasant ride so I stayed on it, figuring my usual on-the-fly routing that had been working so well for the past three weeks would continue to lead me on the right path to my destination.

Crossing into Vicksburg on the east shore of the Mississippi River brought back a memory of one of the most painful days of my adult life—the day that started the downward spiral that eventually led me to explore my childhood and the influence it has on my life today and put me on my current journey of recovery. There is a Walmart in Vicksburg, visible on the south side from I-20, where, on a cold, rainy Monday morning in November of 2002 while I was delivering a motorcycle to a friend who had moved from Miami to Utah, I was—over the phone—brutally fired from the most important job I've ever had.

Probably the most harmful thing, out of thousands of put downs, slights, and insults my dad ever said to me was what he said the day I came home from a Boy Scout field trip to a Coast Guard icebreaker, the Northwind, when I was still in elementary school.

I rushed into the house, excited and sure of myself: "Dad, I know what I want to do when I grow up! I want to join the Coast Guard!"

"The Coast Guard will never take anybody like you," was his reply. "The Coast Guard only wants good people."

I tried to argue with him and convince him I could become "good" and the Coast Guard would take me when I grew up, but he was adamant that it was impossible for me.

I've carried the weight of that statement with me all my life. I knew he was wrong, but always lived my life as if he were right.

It was just one of many similar conversations—one of the thousands of those Chihuahua bites—but this one tore some sort of a psychological Achilles heel and hobbled me for most of my life. I can think of dozens of times over the years I'd apply for a job I really wanted, fill out the application, then slink out the back door with my head hanging low and throw away the application without turning it in because I knew no place would hire "somebody like me." Or if I did turn it in and get an interview, I wouldn't show up.

Later, when I was graduating from high school and should have been thinking about going to college, dad's advice was to get a job as a baggage handler for an airline. "That'd be a good career for you."

I didn't want to settle for a job as a career, but I didn't have the confidence to attempt what I knew I was capable of, so I worked at a series of no-future jobs: construction, factory work, commercial fishing, truck driving, warehouse work, bartending; and I'd always do well at them, but they were never anything I wanted to stay at.

I was forty years old and had thirteen years of recovery before I developed enough confidence in myself to go to school for a career I wanted. I studied journalism and did well and felt like I was finally achieving something I always thought I was capable of, but had been afraid to try. I felt like I'd finally shaken a heavy, burdensome load.

Before I finished at the university, I had—as a freelancer— begun writing a weekly motorcycle column for a major newspaper in Miami; from that, an editor from a high-end lifestyle magazine contacted me and asked me to write for him. Then I began to work for one of the top national newspapers reporting big stories: the terror attacks on the World Trade Center, Anthrax, the shoe bomber, Florida election fiascos, and many more important issues from that time.

My work was good and I felt good. But a part of me always felt like an imposter: *"If they only knew who I really am, they wouldn't let me work here,"* was a constant underlying thought. And my attempts to compensate for my insecurities and fears—and my father's voice—put me in such an awkward, defensive position that I couldn't handle the social and interpersonal aspects of the profession. My attempts to compensate for my own poor self-image backfired, and the work with the major newspaper ended on the end of a cell phone in the rain outside a Walmart in Vicksburg. After that I regressed; my dad's voice was replaced by my own saying, "Dad was right."

Two years later my little sister died about the time all my freelance work dried up, and I just didn't have the strength to keep fighting for more. My world got very small and dark for a lot of years.

I thought about pulling off and stopping at the Walmart and looking at the spot where I took that call, but decided this is one of those object fixation situations I'm better off looking past. I kept going.

Farther east down the interstate I noticed a road sign at an exit pointing north toward the town of Philadelphia, Mississippi, which brought up thoughts of my mother again. After my grandmother died, my mom looked for her father, whom she had never met. She had fabulous luck and located his family in Philadelphia within a couple weeks of starting her search. He had died a number of years prior, but she had three half-sisters, whom she immediately connected and bonded with, and a large extended family that welcomed her as long lost family with all the love, hospitality, and grace anyone could hope for. She located a missing part of herself there in Mississippi and was able to begin healing a deep, lifelong wound that she had sought, but failed, to cure with her mother's help.

She found a path to recovery with her newly discovered family.

I'm finding my path to recovery through the Twelve Steps with a fellowship of people who understand how a short conversation with my father forty-some years ago can have such an effect on me today. In fact, trying to share those feelings with my boss is what led to that phone call. I thought we had a strong enough friendship that I could open up about those things. I was asking for her help, but opening up and asking for help from people who are not prepared to give it, from people who don't understand, just sounds like complaining to them. It hit her the wrong way at the wrong time, and it cost me dearly.

Finally, I turned south off I-20 onto 145, an alternative bypass around the city of Meridian, Mississippi that tied into US Route 45, which would take me down to I-10 in Mobile, Alabama. The bypass was a rural two-laner and I thought, "This is a nice way to spend the last hundred miles before the all-interstate push from Mobile to home." Then, when the bypass joined the actual highway and turned into a four-lane divided highway I thought, "This is good; I can make better time this way." At the Alabama State Line, Route 45 reverted back to two lanes and I happily readjusted again. The funk I'd picked up in Arkansas was long behind, and I'd managed to leave all the old Vicksburg trauma in Vicksburg. I was riding free and easy with the anticipation of seeing my wife soon and was fully enjoying the ride. Whatever the road offered was fine by me as long as I was putting on miles.

I made my last gas-and-snack stop before Mobile in the little unincorporated town of Kushla, Alabama, where I nibbled on some food and drank a liter of water while leaning against a tree in an empty field next to the gas station and admired the filthy, bug-splattered bike that had carried me through more than half this country's states. I asked a lady to snap a photo of me next to it before heading back onto the road.

Only a few miles later I began noticing cars in the oncoming lane with their headlights on—a sure sign that rain was close ahead; then a few cars came toward me with their wipers still running; and, as I got closer to the coast, the sky turned ugly with thick, black, low clouds. I stopped and put on my raingear.

LAST STOP IN ALABAMA BEFORE THE MAD PUSH FOR HOME

I hit Mobile and a hard but sporadic rain at the same time. Traffic was heavy and slow through the city center, not fast enough to blow the water off my face shield or keep it from fogging up on the inside, so I had to ride with it open and stay ducked down below the raised windshield. I-10 passes through a tunnel under the Mobile River, then over an eight-mile-long bridge over Mobile Bay before crossing into Florida. Although I managed to stay relaxed amongst the traffic, my pace wasn't. I was in full combat-commuting mode. Taking advantage of my small size and quick acceleration, I darted in and out of whatever lane was moving the quickest. Getting home as efficiently as possible was my only objective. I'd checked the mileage from my last stop and figured on two more stops for gas; I had just enough small bills in my wallet to cover a McDonald's stop and tolls on the turnpike. Allowing for a short nap at a rest area somewhere along the way, I planned on getting home not long after midnight.

Traffic lightened once I got past the bridge, but at the Florida border I rode into the tropical system the Weather Channel had warned me about and hit a wall of water as thick as any I've ever ridden through. I'm sure there are waterfalls that don't drop as much water as that storm did. It was the kind of rain where vehicles were stopping under overpasses and those that were still moving had their four-way flashers on and most slowed down to thirty or forty miles per hour.

My strategy in heavy rain is to keep going but stay as far away from other vehicles as possible. My gear keeps me dry, warm, and comfortable; I trust my bike and my skill and never ride with worn tires. I have control over myself and the bike, but not over the other drivers in their warm, insulated cars full of distractions. With only a single taillight, my biggest fear is of becoming invisible in the mist kicked up behind my tire and getting plowed into by an inattentive driver, so I tend to ride faster than traffic. Not stupid fast, but just enough so that I'm in control of my surroundings.

I-10 through the Florida panhandle is mostly two lanes each direction, and I got caught behind a pair of cars that stayed side-by-side at forty miles per hour for a long distance. I guess they felt safe seeing clear road ahead, but if they'd bothered checking their mirrors, they would have seen a lot of traffic jammed up behind. With these two idiots ahead and a bunch of cars behind, I felt like a potential piece of meat in a cage-'n-bike sandwich. Neither car would respond to my flashing headlight and accelerate enough to make a gap for me to slide past. I was getting impatient and pissed off at these guys and riding too close, trying to force one of them to move—not a good mindset. I had no control over them and was losing control over myself; I wasn't relaxed anymore—not a safe way to ride. The smartest thing to do was to pull off the road and let the whole cluster get far enough ahead that I wouldn't be stuck in the pack, so I took the next exit, ate an early dinner, and let myself relax a bit even though it cost me time I didn't want to waste. That's all I had control over—me—and I'm here now, so it was the right decision.

If I were one who believed in signs I would have turned around and left Florida as fast as possible after my next gas stop.

I was keeping a close watch on the fuel gauge, wanting to get as much distance out of the tank before filling in order to keep the stops to a minimum, so when I did eventually stop just east of Tallahassee I really needed gas.

Usually on a trip like this, somewhere on the second or third day my credit card will be denied at a gas station for suspicious activity and I'll have to call the company and verify that it is me using the card and explain why I'm making so many small purchases every few hours. But on this trip, the gods of plastic commerce waited until the twenty-second day—two stops from home—to figure out my spending habits had changed and, for my protection, put a hold on the card. I was pissed. The station I was at didn't have a convenient place to get out from the rain so I didn't want to call from there, but I was so low on gas that I didn't dare ride on to find a more hospitable location. I ended up spending all my handy cash for a partial tank and rode on till I could stop at a rest area to clear up the "fraud alert" over the phone. That cost me another hour and it was dark by the time I got going again.

I'd just enjoyed three trouble-free weeks on the road, and now, within the first few hours after entering my home state I'd ridden through some of the worst rain I've ever experienced, been scared enough by traffic that I'd pulled off the road (for only the second time in my life), and been fucked with by my credit card company. It didn't feel very welcoming.

Despite that unfavorable welcome, I continued. The rain eventually lessened and I turned south onto I-75 and ran down to Gainesville where I stopped at a Cracker Barrel restaurant and ordered a bowl of soup just to break a hundred dollar bill so I'd have proper change for the tolls on the turnpike.

Returning late at night is my favorite way to end a trip. It's easy to ignore how boring and tedious riding through Florida is when it's dark, the traffic is light, and rest areas are empty enough that it's possible to find a quiet place to take a short, undisturbed nap, which I did in a booth at a restaurant at a service plaza on the turnpike. I needed to make an extra fuel stop because of the glitch with the credit card—in all, that glitch, and the subsequent complications, had added about three hours to the day's ride.

I rolled into my driveway just after daybreak and was welcomed by two rambunctious dogs and a loving wife.

It was good to be home again. The trip was over, but the journey continues.

HOME

MY FIRST FEW DAYS back home were spent catching up with domestic duties. Summer grass grows astonishingly fast in Miami, and it took me two days to get the lawn back under control. Unloading and cleaning the bike, bathing the dogs, washing the cars, and dozens of other small projects replaced the freedom of only having to decide which direction to ride each morning and when to stop for the night.

Friends who don't ride asked about the trip but were mostly interested in hearing about the dramatic events—camping with dangerous bears and bikers were the favorites. They'd ask a few polite questions, comment on the distance I'd covered in such a short time, and then the conversation would quickly drift back to regular, familiar banter.

Friends who do ride asked about the roads, my equipment and gear, the bike, how well the tires wore, gas prices, logistics, and other details they could use on their own future trips. They were eager to hear the stories and look at photos, but the telling of a trip is a poor substitute for being on the road oneself; it's like the difference between looking at a picture of a campfire and actually feeling the heat of the flames at the end of a long, adventurous day. We'd talk about it for a bit and then reverted back to topics at hand.

The trip had been a solo quest. I'd ridden it alone, for reasons of my own, and I'd accomplished all I'd set out to do.

I had fun and rode to my heart's content. I'd traveled through parts of the country I'd never visited before and seen awe-inspiring mountain ranges and lonesome prairies, sunrises and sunsets, historic rivers, small towns and big cities. I saw wild animals up close, been bored stiff on tedious highways, pushed hard on exhilarating back roads, and experienced the vastness of our great country. I'd made some new friends, caught up with old ones, and had wonderful conversations with strangers.

I'd ridden about ninety-five hundred miles through twenty-seven states and burned through a little more than two hundred gallons of gas, filling the tank fifty-two times. I spent four nights sleeping at friends' places, six in motels, and thirteen on the ground. Most of my meals were fast McDonald's stops—either an Egg McMuffin and a coffee in the morning, or a Quarter Pounder and glass of water for dinner. Small handfuls of raw nuts, beef or buffalo jerky, and lots of water kept me satisfied during the day. I lost twelve pounds—best diet I've ever found.

The bike ran perfectly, needing only regular maintenance. The interstates wore a flat spot in the center of my tires, but they still had plenty of tread left, and, to the trained eye, the roughed-up rubber on the sides of the tires testified to some spirited riding in the twisties.

My time in Seattle and the couple hundred hours I'd spent in the saddle had given me valuable time to reflect on my life. I'd gained some understanding of my upbringing that I'm still digesting, and back at my regular meetings I was able to share those thoughts with people who understand what I'm going through and can offer me helpful feedback. There is a great healing power in that alone.

And, although the trip itself didn't change my life—it was just a segment in my life's continuing journey from then to tomorrow—I'm able to look back with clarity I didn't have before. I can now, with full conviction and without shame, admit that I didn't have a healthy upbringing—and I have a newfound power just by saying that. By taking a long, introspective survey of my life I've gained the freedom and strength to abandon old survival traits that served me back when I was a kid, but have become harmful, lifelong habits and don't suit me well as an adult. I'm gaining the power to change from the inside out so I can stand proud, and, for the first time in my life, with hard-won confidence, define myself as a man of my own making instead of a product of a flawed childhood.

It was good to be able to work on myself among my fellow travelers back home, but the wanderlust was still alive and tugging at me. It only took a few weeks before the road began calling me again. If the trip had been a nourishing meal, I needed dessert.

I had some friends who were racing in the final AMA round of the season at Barber Motorsports Park in Alabama, and I decided the eighteen hundred mile roundtrip ride would be a good weekend getaway.

Along with the world's largest collection of vintage and modern motorcycles in its multi-story museum, Barber may have the most beautiful racetrack in the US. Nestled in the rolling countryside east of Birmingham right off I-20 in the tiny town of Leeds, the track was sculpted out of the land with the vision and care of a master artist. If the combination of speed and competition, the vision of beautiful machinery, and the song of high performance engines could be likened to a precious gem, then Barber Motorsports Park is a setting worthy of the most beautiful of jewels. With large, sloping hills instead of grandstands and thick, manicured grass to sit on instead of hard seats, Barber is a spectator's paradise. I've seen golf courses that look almost industrial compared to Barber's lush landscaping.

The long, hot, torturous ride up the Florida Turnpike to Alabama on the first day of fall was made worse by the seasonal swarm of lovebugs I hit just south of Orlando. They were as thick as the butterflies I'd hit in Kansas, but riding into butterflies is like going into a gentle snowfall; riding into lovebugs is like getting pelted with hundreds of epoxy-filled paintball pellets. They are the nastiest insects I've ever had to clean off the bike; they can ruin the paint and chrome and etch the plastic if left on for any length of time. I had to use an abrasive rag with Clorox to clean them all off the bike once I got to the track the next morning.

The easiest route from Miami to Barber is to head up the turnpike to where it joins I-75 and stay on the interstate until it intersects I-20 in Atlanta, and then go west to Leeds. I wanted to get to the track early Friday morning, so with some time to play, I jumped off 75 at Tifton and took rural roads through Georgia, then stopped for the night at a motel near the Alabama border.

I learned a long time ago to never check in to a motel with a handwritten sign on the front door stating: "No Pennies." I've stayed in a lot of low-end motels on various trips and gathered quite a few funny stories from those stops, and fortunately, I've never had a bad experience. If a place doesn't feel right, I move on to another motel or campground. I've never had harder time finding a place to stay, though, than I did in Columbus, Georgia on US Route 280. I must have checked out a half-dozen motels in that city before giving up and heading on to find a place in the next town. Adding to my no-pennies rule: If a motel has an onsite tattoo parlor—move on; if there are three pawn shops but no restaurants within walking distance to a motel—move on; if there are no cars parked in front of the rooms and the office has a thick, bullet-proof window protecting the manager—move on; if the motel only accepts cash and demands separate deposits for keys and towels—move on; if the motel looks like an episode of *Cops* might have been filmed there—move on. I did, and I'm sure I slept better for it.

The racing was fast and ferocious. Championships were up for grabs with three or four possible winners in four different classes, so the two days of racing were well worth the trip. I helped my friends, John and Barrett Long, in the pits for Barrett's two races, caught up with some other racer friends in the paddock, and tried to make a meeting.

While working as a corner worker at the track during Bike Week in Daytona the previous March, I'd noticed a sign in the paddock from Tim, the AMA Chaplain, announcing a twelve-step meeting for the racers and crew. I spoke to Tim but couldn't make the meeting then because of my on-track duties. I spoke to Tim again at Barber and found out where the meeting was, but again, wasn't able to make it because I was busy packing my tent right after the last race trying to beat a huge tropical storm that was blowing in from the Gulf of Mexico.

TIM

The AMA paddock is a tough, demanding place. Money has been spent. Results are expected. Pressure is heavy. Tension is thick. Add to the mix the daily discipline of recovery from addiction and the pressure increases to the third power.

As the chaplain for AMA Pro Racing, I have seen it all in the paddock—fame, glory, and despair all in a five-minute span. Any tool I can find to assist my job, I'll use to help my "flock."

An AMA team owner, Rob, is in recovery and has been for over two years. Rob is serious about it. His story is real and painful. He has come too far to let it all slip away. Rob approached me after the 2009 season and asked if I would facilitate a twelve-step meeting for racers in recovery. I had attended a twelve-step meeting once. Otherwise, I did not know much of what was involved; however, I told Rob I was in, not sure if it would come to pass.

Before the 2010 season began, I received a call from AMA Pro Racing with the same request. Now I knew it was serious. Behind the request was the desire to have meetings at the track so those in recovery would not have to spend time they did not have looking for meetings in the cities where we race.

The first meeting was scheduled for Daytona during Bike Week. The meeting was publicized, a contact number distributed…and two guys showed up, Rob and a corner worker who couldn't stay because he had to get back to his station. Surprisingly neither Rob nor I were discouraged. We recognized the growing pains and made plans for the next meeting in Fontana, California, just Rob and me.

We moved on, and as the season progressed and word got out, we began to get more and more people. At Road Atlanta we had three, at Infineon, California, three. Mid-Ohio saw four, including a new person who had just completed rehab and wanted to attach himself to a meeting. By the time AMA Pro Racing got to our annual stop at Virginia International Raceway, we had five, all men, who were affiliated with our twelve-step meeting.

The stories were a cross between heartbreaking and material for reality television. These men had been addicted to everything from cocaine to sex. They maintained their recovery by a daily discipline of serenity, prayer, and a dependence on God.

The best meeting, for me, was hearing Simeon, an older man in recovery for twenty-eight years, tell a younger man who was struggling to simply "Trust in God." I, too, needed that reminder, as my wife had recently suffered an injury that would leave her unable to work for five months.

We ended the season at Barber Motorsports Park in Alabama with four men. One of our members had relapsed and we were all concerned for him. After the meeting ended, Rob and I evaluated our first year and were pleased with what we saw and experienced.

Our plans for the 2011 season are to continue as we did in 2010, one day at a time, one race at a time, depending on God to lead us to others who need and desire the support and accountability a twelve-step program provides.

I got on the road about six in the evening with the first sporadic raindrops from the storm dropping out of the darkening sky and hitting my windshield. I decided to use the interstate, rather than get caught on a rural road in a heavy storm, and made it to Atlanta before the weather hit hard just as twilight faded into complete darkness.

This storm was worse than the one that greeted me when I entered Florida from the long trip; I didn't see another motorcycle on the road the entire night. Two things kept me going: I was desperate to get past Orlando before the lovebugs came out for their mid-morning onslaught, and I figured it was, even in the storm, safer to ride at night when the traffic would be lighter than during the daytime when all the regular drivers would be commuting in such terrible weather. I hit one puddle on the highway that I couldn't see beforehand in the darkness that was so deep that the water coming off my front tire knocked my feet off the pegs, and once I saw a flash of light ahead of me that I thought was lightning (I would have stopped and found shelter in a lightning storm), but it turned out to be a semi-truck spinning out and jackknifing in the center lane.

By the time I made the Florida border, I'd ridden out of the storm and found a picnic table in a rest area just north of Gainesville to catch a couple hours of sleep. I beat the lovebugs near Orlando and made it home just as my wife was leaving for work on Monday morning.

As fall stretched its way to winter and the days grew short, my riding was restricted to South Florida. Other than getting together with my regular riding buddies for our Thursday night dinner ride, I didn't spend much time on the bike. I did get invited by a friend named Cajun Joe to ride along with the Alternative MC, a clean and sober club out of Delray Beach, on their annual Christmas Run to a home for kids who are waiting to be adopted.

That was my second ride with the club. I'd joined them earlier in the year at a memorial service for "Dad," one of their founding members and a Viet Nam Veteran who'd passed away after a long battle with the lingering effects from exposure to Agent Orange.

Going from the clubhouse to the service was my first time riding in "pack formation" with a large group, and it was a powerful, seductive experience. We rode side-by-side with about a bike's-length distance between us fore and aft. It takes faith in everyone's ability to ride that close, and that's one of the reasons clubs have a probationary period before a prospective member becomes a full patch holder. These guys knew each other and had been riding together for a long time, and the pack operated like a single entity. There were probably somewhere around thirty of us—I was the unknown, and so, as there was an odd number of riders, was assigned a position alone in the second to last row. At intersections two riders stopped cross traffic so we could all make it safely through together. On the freeway the lead rider, the Road Captain, would signal a lane change, then the two riders in the back of the pack would be the first to move over— to keep traffic from coming up into the middle of the pack—then the next row would move over, followed by the next in line, with the leaders being the last to take their positions in the new lane. It was all done with military-like precision, like a well-practiced marching band in a parade, but its loud growling dirge was played out of chromed exhaust pipes instead of brass tubas, trumpets, and trombones.

The service brought riders in from all over the Southeast. There were members from at least three different clubs paying respects to a fallen brother. Cajun Joe told me about how Dad had lost his hearing toward the end, so club members would take him to meetings and write down what was said so he could follow along, keeping him in the group and keeping his recovery active. Joe also told me about how, when he'd been in a bad accident and spent time in the hospital, Dad and the rest of the club members paid his rent and rebuilt his bike so he could ride as soon as his body allowed.

The club is an extended family, often much stronger and much more supportive than a member's real family had been.

Another member named "Cadillac" had passed away a couple years before, and the club took on the responsibility of paying for his kid's education, making personal contributions and holding fundraisers in order to pay for college tuition.

I was sitting at the clubhouse one night talking with a couple guys when a homeless drunk lady wandered in asking for spare change and a cigarette. She didn't know what she was getting into.

A few guys took her aside and talked to her, asking if she wanted help. Within an hour after she asked for it, they found her a bed in a detox facility and someone drove her to treatment—and gave her the cigarette.

For the Christmas run the club had raised almost ten thousand dollars to donate to the individual kids, to the families of kids who have been adopted, and to the center itself. More than a hundred kids got a Christmas that they would not have had if it weren't for a small chapter of recovering bikers. It was a real honor to be a part of it.

The day ended with a "burnout," where Joe and "Nudge" lit up their rear tires to the thrill all of the kids under the watchful eye of Santa.

BURNOUT FOR THE KIDS AND SANTA

My recovery is a true gift that was first given to suffering drunks in Akron seventy-some years ago, and has been passed down and expanded through a worldwide fellowship that has grown to include anyone needing guidance to change their lives. The Twelve Steps are a map of last resort out of desperation. I had been lost in addiction and found my way out, and when I got lost again in the lingering effects of an unhealthy childhood the steps still worked as my guide to a healthy life, and I found another fellowship of travelers on the same path to join me in my journey.

And on two wheels I found a fellowship of recovery, adventure, motion, speed, creativity, family, solitude, rebellion, and gratitude. I believe those of us who navigate our way through recovery on two wheels are doubly blessed. I know I am.

ACKNOWLEDGMENTS

TO MY LOVING WIFE Zaydee, for understanding my need to ride—sometimes far and sometimes fast—and allowing me the time and freedom to do so. To Bob for giving me the opportunity to write this book, and to Nancy and Valerie for tolerating so many missed deadlines. To Alan Troop, a fellow writer and solid friend, and David Schroeder who taught me so much about writing in two short semesters at community college. To Bob, Dan, Gordon, Tom, and the rest of the Thursday night riding group for the camaraderie, and to John Long for introducing me to the track. To my fellow travelers in the Coming Out of the Weeds group—I owe you my life. And finally to the crew at Starbucks in Coconut Grove for keeping my typing fingers lubricated with all that Pike Place Roast.